Introducing Shakespeare's Comedies, Histories, and Romances

Introducing Shakespeare's Comedies, Histories, and Romances

A Guide for Teachers

Victor L. Cahn

ROWMAN & LITTLEFIELD
Lanham • Boulder • New York • London

Published by Rowman & Littlefield
A wholly owned subsidiary of The Rowman & Littlefield Publishing Group, Inc.
4501 Forbes Boulevard, Suite 200, Lanham, Maryland 20706
www.rowman.com

Unit A, Whitacre Mews, 26-34 Stannary Street, London SE11 4AB

Copyright © 2017 by Victor L. Cahn

All rights reserved. No part of this book may be reproduced in any form or by any electronic or mechanical means, including information storage and retrieval systems, without written permission from the publisher, except by a reviewer who may quote passages in a review.

British Library Cataloguing in Publication Information Available

Library of Congress Cataloging-in-Publication Data

Names: Cahn, Victor L. author.
Title: Introducing Shakespeare's comedies, histories, and romances : a guide for teachers / Victor L. Cahn.
Description: Lanham : Rowman & Littlefield, 2017. | Includes bibliographical references.
Identifiers: LCCN 2017019727 (print) | LCCN 2017030876 (ebook) | ISBN 9781475838008 (electronic) | ISBN 9781475837988 (cloth : alk. paper) | ISBN 9781475837995 (pbk. : alk. paper)
Subjects: LCSH: Shakespeare, William, 1564–1616—Study and teaching.
Classification: LCC PR2987 (ebook) | LCC PR2987 .C275 2017 (print) | DDC 822.3/3—dc23 LC record available at https://lccn.loc.gov/2017019727

Printed in the United States of America

To the memory of my mother,
Evelyn Baum Cahn,
who taught these plays many years ago.

Contents

Preface	ix
Introduction	xi
A Few Words About the Comedies	1
1 *The Taming of the Shrew*	3
2 *A Midsummer Night's Dream*	15
3 *The Merchant of Venice*	25
4 *Twelfth Night*, or *What You Will*	37
A Few Words About the Histories	49
5 *Richard II*	53
6 *Henry IV, Part 1*	67
A Few Words About the Romances	81
7 *The Tempest*	83
Afterword	95
About the Author	97

Preface

For forty years I taught the plays of Shakespeare, and the more I taught and wrote about them, the more fascinating they became. Now I'd like to share some of what I learned with my fellow instructors, in the hope of aiding those at the junior high school, high school, and undergraduate levels who offer some of Shakespeare's most familiar works to students who are largely unfamiliar with them.

I've divided my material into two books: one on the tragedies, the other on the comedies, histories, and romances. Each volume begins with a general introduction intended for any teacher preparing to present any play in the canon. This section includes biographical material on Shakespeare, information about the world of the theater in which he flourished, and perspective on the intellectual underpinnings of his time. Not everything here will be appropriate for every instructor, but I like to think that most will find something of value in my cursory overview.

I then move to a baker's dozen of Shakespeare's plays, all of which have inspired enthusiastic response from classes. Although I assume that my readers have already experienced the works, I proceed through each as if an audience was encountering it for the first time. Because these analyses can only broach the wealth of discussion suggested by the texts, my strategy is to propose what actors and directors sometimes refer to as the "spine" of the play: an overarching conflict or motivation that I embellish with specifics. Thus when quoting, I rarely reprint entire passages. Instead I focus on crucial sections and trust that my colleagues will help students delve more deeply.

This effort leads to the most challenging aspect of Shakespeare's plays: the language. Both the poetry and prose are extraordinary but also multilayered and sometimes archaic, and students are likely to be unaccustomed to probing words as closely as Shakespeare demands. As a result, many will resort to editions in which the dialogue is "translated" into modern English, but part of our job is to ensure that even those who avail themselves of such tools still appreciate the original.

Therefore, during sessions students should keep the text in front of them, and teachers should constantly direct attention to specific lines. These should be read out loud, by either the instructor or the students, because Shakespeare's words were meant to be heard, not seen. In addition, even though we devote considerable class time to explicating this complex material, students still deserve assurance that even if they (like almost all of us) don't understand every word, they can still grasp the beauty and power of Shakespeare's writing.

My overall aim is to analyze how these plays succeed as theater. Decades ago, to help achieve that end, I brought recordings to class, then in later years moved to VHSs and DVDs. Now multiple performances are available on the web, and all of us can watch at our own convenience. I still suggest, though, that students first read the play under discussion, then turn to a video because the combination of sight and sound should make the deepest impression. No doubt these plays are most effective in performance, but I'm also convinced that under the guidance of a skillful teacher, they may prove compelling in the classroom, as well.

All quotations are taken from the Folger Shakespeare Library editions.

My thanks to Tom Koerner and Emily Tuttle of Rowman & Littlefield, who have supported this project from the start, as well as my production editor, Lara Hahn, who diligently prepared the manuscript.

My gratitude as always to my brother, Dr. Steven M. Cahn, my trusted guide on all matters scholarly and otherwise.

Introduction

William Shakespeare was above all a man of the theater, and he was fortunate that his creative life coincided with an era when English drama thrived. His oeuvre, though, was part of a tradition that extended back through the Middle Ages, when plays were presented by itinerant performers. Gradually these groups were replaced by professional companies, stimulated by the ever-growing market for entertainment in London, the capital of the country and its economic, political, and social center.

Theater of that time benefitted from a confluence of other forces. By 1558, when Elizabeth I ascended the throne, the spirit of the Renaissance had brought renewed interest in classical literature, specifically Roman playwrights like Terence and Plautus, writers of comedy, and Seneca, author of numerous tragedies, and these figures became models for young dramatists. Furthermore, professional companies were sanctioned, while theater continued to burgeon in academic institutions and private halls. Public performances were given in innyards, where galleries were built to hold spectators.

These companies were infused with university graduates, most notably Christopher Marlowe, like Shakespeare born in 1564. The author of several masterpieces, including *Dr. Faustus*, Marlowe spent his life in notorious circles and was killed in a tavern brawl before the age of thirty. Nevertheless, his distinctive variety of blank verse, sometimes called the "mighty line," contributed enormously to the poetic style that shaped drama, including Shakespeare's, for decades.

Meanwhile, acting companies remained under attack by the Puritans, who condemned theater not only because it ostensibly contributed to moral dissolution but also because performances interfered with business. In addition, given that theater companies functioned in unsavory areas, the lord mayor and his counsel objected for reasons of both health and decorum. Thus in

1574, decrees were passed so that no plays could be presented within city limits unless scripts, as well as times and places of performance, were officially approved. In reaction, acting companies built playhouses just outside the municipality, and here they prospered until 1642, when the Puritans closed operations entirely.

Shakespeare joined this world in approximately 1590, when he was in his mid-twenties. His own education had been limited to grammar school in his birthplace of Stratford, where he was one of eight children born to John and Mary Shakespeare. John was a glover who enjoyed some good fortune but also suffered severe financial setbacks, so young Shakespeare must have known both a degree of comfort as well as the pangs and humiliations of poverty. He also seems to have had a remarkable memory for the sights, sounds, and smells of his hometown.

By the way, members of the group known as the anti-Stratfordians claim that the individual known as William Shakespeare could not have written the body of work attributed to him. The primary reason is that an untutored fellow was incapable of producing such masterpieces, and among the other candidates are the Earl of Oxford, Marlowe, and Queen Elizabeth herself. Without going into the vast body of evidence that supports the view that the man from Stratford wrote these plays (notably that almost everybody else proposed as author was dead when the works appeared), let's assume that they are his and move on.

As a schoolboy, William endured lengthy hours in a classroom whose curriculum was heavily weighted with Latin literature, including writings of Cicero, Horace, Virgil, and Ovid, and proof of such study may be found throughout Shakespeare's writings. Recitation was a bulwark of instruction, and no doubt emphasis on articulation and rhythmic precision gave Shakespeare affection for both the glories of language and the delights of performance. He also read intensively in Roman history, and some of the lessons he learned emerge in his Roman plays and his sequences about English history.

In 1582, Shakespeare married Anne Hathaway, eight years his senior and several months pregnant with their first child. Within three years, the couple had three children: Susanna, born in 1583, and twins Hamnet and Judith, born in 1585. Hamnet would die at age eleven. The seven years following the birth of his twins are the so-called lost years because documentary evidence about Shakespeare's activities is limited. Speculation holds that he may have been a schoolmaster, a provincial actor, or a lawyer's assistant. He may also have spent time on the Continent.

By 1592, however, he must have been established in London, for he was alluded to disparagingly by playwright Robert Greene. In an attack on actors in general, Greene refers to "Shake-scene," then to an "upstart crow" with "his Tyger's hart wrapt in a Player's hyde [sic]."

The last parodies a line from *Henry VI, Part 3*: "O, tiger's heart wrapped in a woman's hide" (1, 4, 140). Greene may have been intimating that Shakespeare was a plagiarist or merely that the young man was presumptuous. Whatever the implication, the reference shows that Shakespeare was well known enough to be obliquely criticized.

In 1592, an outbreak of bubonic plague struck the city, and for two years theaters were closed. When they reopened in 1594, Shakespeare, as actor and playwright, joined a new company called the Lord Chamberlain's Men under the auspices of an aristocratic personage who provided artistic and economic protection. During the rest of the 1590s, the company rented theaters, but by 1599 the Globe Theater had been constructed, and here is where most performances of Shakespeare's plays were presented. In 1623, after James I became king, the name was changed to the King's Men.

Thus for a substantial time Shakespeare enjoyed a creative environment that playwrights have always relished: the opportunity to write for a resident company of capable and experienced actors, with their own facilities at the ready. Had he lived in another era, he might have written 154 sonnets and several longer poems, but he almost certainly would not have written the 37 plays that remain celebrated.

Theatrical conditions helped shape the dramatic works of this day. In most theaters, the stage, a covered platform without curtains, extended into the audience. Toward the rear of the stage was a higher level that could serve as a balcony or "battlement," from which actors could look down on the action below. Most of the theaters were open-air constructions, round or hexagonal, and of considerable size. The Globe itself could hold two thousand spectators. Yet the houses encouraged intimacy between audience and actor, so that asides and soliloquies became a valuable method of communication.

In most public theaters, two or three tiers of seats were provided for the well-to-do, who sometimes overflowed onto the stage. Here they tended to behave somewhat disreputably in an effort to draw attention to themselves. Below the stage, in the pit, stood or sat the less wealthy citizens, known as the "groundlings," and they were an impatient, demanding group. Yet they were also appreciative and, when moved by what they saw and heard, were prone to cheering, shouting, and crying.

Perhaps because Shakespeare's audience encompassed so wide a range of people, he created equally heterogeneous rosters of characters, from the highest echelons of society to the very bottom, and placed them in a variety of locales, settings, and moods. He also moved regularly from comedy to history to tragedy, triumphing in each form with a virtuosity unmatched by any other dramatist before or since.

Most of Shakespeare's works were written for public theaters, and their technical deficiencies also influenced his writing. Perhaps needless to say, artificial lighting was not available, so performances took place in the daytime and without intermissions. Division of the plays into separate acts was accomplished by later editors, and therefore audience attention must have been considerable. Granted, few other entertainments were available: church services, executions, and bear baiting, to name some of the most prominent. Thus theater was a welcome alternative. Nonetheless, to hold audience focus, a premium was placed on continual action.

Costumes were extravagant and helped define character in terms of nationality and class. Scenery, however, was minimal, and flats, curtains, and simple wooden structures had to suffice to represent houses and other edifices. Props were strictly for efficacy. Programs were not available, so the text itself had to identify characters and establish locales. Hence Shakespeare's poetic renderings of environment were not just for the sake of beauty but also to communicate the texture of a forest or castle that had to be suggested rather than re-created.

Battles between massive armies were enacted by a few performers dashing about the stage with swords. Although trapdoors and such devices as sound and visual effects were available to simulate supernatural and other spectacular displays, the unceasing movement in Shakespeare's plays, the energy we as yet admire, was demanded by the conditions under which he worked.

Theatrical conditions also imposed demands on the actors. The turnover of plays was steady, and parts had to be learned after only a few rehearsals and with little direction (and while actors were performing in other works). Thus their capacity for memorization must have been astonishing. Yet we should remember the nature of elementary education in England at this time. The primary activity was rote training, and at a very early age students were drilled into retaining long poems and prose passages. (For confirmation, ask your students how many remember whatever material they memorized during their initial academic years.)

Acting itself was carried out with vigor and passion, tending toward the declamatory. Again, to state the obvious, no microphones or other methods for projection were available. Indeed, Shakespeare's taste for what in our day would be described as "chewing the scenery" may be seen in Hamlet's instructions to the players in 3, 2. The most famous members of Shakespeare's company were Richard Burbage, who gave the premiere performances of most of Shakespeare's great tragic roles, and Will Kemp, a gifted comic star whose liberties onstage antagonized his colleagues and led to his dismissal.

Shakespeare himself also appeared onstage, generally in smaller roles and often as older men. He may have been the Chorus in *Henry V*, apologizing for the limits of his writing, and he may have played the Ghost in *Hamlet*. No matter the extent of his contributions as a thespian, however; his primary task was to write, and he did so with unmatched success. Contemporary reports indicate that productions of his works were successful and that no matter his actors' deficiencies, Shakespeare was well served.

The most important limitation on the playwright was the absence of actresses. Although women were permitted to perform on the Continent, the English judged such practice as immoral, and from medieval times all female roles were played by boys. One consequence of this restriction was that the parts Shakespeare wrote for males outnumber those for females by five or six to one.

A couple of these boys must have been talented, for many of Shakespeare's comedies contain prominent roles for pairs of young women. In addition, Shakespeare frequently arranges for one or both to disguise themselves as men. The impersonation is always successful, but even given that ploy, the capacity of his audience to accept the illusion of boys playing girls must have been remarkable.

To be sure, the plays generally lack extended female parts, especially for mature women, because boys could not carry off a role as complex as Othello or Lear. Late in his career, however, Shakespeare must have found at least one young male in whom he had confidence because he created Lady Macbeth, Cleopatra, and other roles whose demands match those of his greatest male parts.

For nearly twenty years, from the early 1590s until 1611, Shakespeare wrote an average of two plays a year, and the steadiness of his output suggests that he had little time for revision. Thus what have been passed down to us may not be precisely first drafts, but surely the speeches and pages flowed easily from his quill. In contrast to later dramatists, Shakespeare wrote strictly for performance and most likely without an eye toward publication. In fact, only about half his plays were printed individually during his lifetime.

The playwright seems to have paid little attention to textual accuracy. Laws of the day gave him no copyright control, so prompters, actors, other playwrights, and even company bookkeepers could make changes that satisfied their needs. Besides, once plays were published, they were no longer the province of an individual company, which would lose a valuable commodity when a popular script was available to rival groups.

Fortunately, in 1623, seven years after Shakespeare's death, two of his former colleagues collected thirty-six of his plays in a single volume known as the First Folio (*Pericles* is omitted). Here the plays are classified as tragedies, histories, and comedies. This text is the basis for virtually all editions currently used, but innumerable questions about authenticity remain. Many different editors worked on the volume, so some copies of the folio are at variance with others. Words, stage directions, spelling, and even entire passages are all open to question.

No single book on Shakespeare can encompass all perspectives from which the plays may be considered. This book is based on a traditional conviction: that the core of their impact lies with the characters. So lifelike are they that although they are set in ages long past, we are inspired to explore them as we would real human beings. We may struggle to resolve some of their seemingly contradictory actions and statements, but these can almost always be synthesized into what actors designate as a "through line," a consistent path of motivation.

Dramatic figures, like people, reveal themselves through language and action. We analyze them not only by what they do but also by what they say and how they say it. Two precepts apply here. One, the language a speaker uses, taken in concert with the speaker's actions, reveals the speaker's character, while the richness of the language reflects the depth of that character. Two, how that character reacts to circumstances of plot reveals theme.

Attempting to analyze language in these plays can be daunting. First, many of Shakespeare's words are no longer part of our vocabulary. Second, other words seem familiar, but their meaning may have changed drastically since he penned them. Third, pronunciation may also have altered, so that we are not aware of potential homonyms (words that sound alike) or puns. Fourth, to enrich his dialogue, Shakespeare uses not only metaphors and similes, as well as numerous other forms of imagery, but also a variety of poetic and rhetorical devices that can make the immediate meaning problematic.

Individual lines can also create difficulties. Roughly three-quarters of Shakespeare's dialogue is blank verse or unrhymed iambic pentameter. An iamb consists of one short syllable followed by one long one or one unaccented syllable followed by one accented one; for example, "da-DUM." Pentameter refers to a line with five such beats. Sometimes the iambic verse is rhymed, usually when the speaker wants to project artificiality. Thus rhymed couplets appear in asides, declarations of love, or other contexts requiring a linguistic flair. Speakers may also use prose, which is offered in less formal circumstances or by less exalted characters.

We should remember that although Shakespeare's characters reveal aspects of humanity at large, they themselves function during a specific time and in a specific place. Thus they should be seen as reflecting aspects of the culture in which they were created. Elizabethan England was primarily Christian, and its view of the world followed generally from a medieval vision. This held that the universe was created by God as a perfect work, a unity in which every aspect of creation had its place.

This "great chain of being" encompassed all, from the lowest inanimate objects to the angels, placing each in what were judged to be natural places of subordination. Humankind occupied a unique place, for the human animal possessed both soul and body and therefore endured a conflict between its divine capacity, or reason, and its base appetites, or passions. Any imperfections in the world were caused by humanity, not God.

Within this system was a series of correspondences. As God was the highest among the angels, so the sun was the highest among the stars, fire the highest of the elements, the king the highest among human beings, and so on. In addition, a fundamental relationship existed between the macrocosm and the microcosm. God was ruler of the universe, the macrocosm, as a monarch was ruler of the political structure, the microcosm. Any disorder in the social microcosm created repercussions that extended into the macrocosm.

Order in the political realm corresponded to order in the human body. Just as the surrounding world, the macrocosm, was said to be composed of four elements (fire, air, water, and earth), so the human microcosm contained four parallel humors (choler, blood, phlegm, and melancholy). Any imbalance of these within an individual could lead to disorder that extended into the political plane and even into the universal plane. Finally, we have to keep in mind that this medieval vision was tempered by the influence of the Renaissance and the Reformation.

The Renaissance (literally, "rebirth") was an age during which leading thinkers believed they were inspiring a return to the human and earthly concerns of the pagan classical world. In addition to celebrating this artistic heritage, the fourteenth and fifteenth centuries saw the development of a money economy, with increased opportunity for individual trade and profit. At the same time, urban populations grew, and intellectual life in the universities expanded, while scientific inquiry and a resultant skepticism emerged.

The European Reformation, based primarily on religious motives, took some authority away from the church by insisting on a personal relationship between each human being and God. In England, the Reformation followed Henry VIII's rift with the Catholic Church over his divorce. Attendance in the new Church of England was still enforced, but now the English monarch also held authority over religious matters, and the psychological fulcrum that the Catholic Church had provided for centuries was splintered.

These two powerful movements held some conflicting values. While the Renaissance reveled in the possibilities of secular daily life, the Reformation emphasized individual piety and an overwhelming concern for the afterlife. Renaissance humanism judged human nature to be fundamentally benign, while according to the Reformation, humanity was essentially depraved. The Renaissance advocated reason; the Reformation sought to impose faith and conformity.

Yet the Renaissance and Reformation had equally important values in common. Both emerged from a mercantile system based on capitalism and an ever-developing and prosperous middle class. Both shook the image of the world as a static entity, and each in its own way shifted responsibility toward the individual. This new perspective gave rise to new freedoms but also to new uncertainties.

In England, the rise of the gentry reflected alienation from a feudal system to one based on private enterprise. The nation was beset by a series of intellectual and moral crises springing from disputes over political rights, social rights, and the seemingly heretical results of scientific discovery, such as those by Copernicus and Galileo. In addition, awareness of new lands and societies, especially throughout the Americas, caused European civilization to reflect on the very nature of the human species, as well as on fundamental questions of morality and theology.

All this turmoil was reflected in the central subject of Elizabethan literature: the struggle for stability between individual lives and the social order. Shakespeare's plays, too, dramatize this tension between old and new, between the world as a closed, structured system and the power of individuals to find their own way. The plays celebrate individuality but at the same time reflect the belief that the assertion of an individual's will creates conflict. For when that will is exercised, whether in the malevolent desire for power or wealth or a beneficent desire for love, equilibrium within the individual is upset.

This imbalance in Shakespeare's characters is always the mainspring of the plot, the force that propels the action. In the comedies and certain romances, personal imbalance tends to remain localized. In Shakespeare's tragedies, histories, and other romances, it occurs within individuals of such magnitude that their actions have ramifications that spread throughout the social, political, and even universal structure.

Virtually all of Shakespeare's plots are borrowed from earlier sources. Whatever the story, though, all of Shakespeare's plays end with the reestablishment of personal and political order. Such restoration reflects the essential conservatism of both the age and the playwright, but Shakespeare's conservatism is profoundly humanitarian. Even at his most pessimistic, when cruelty and heartbreak seem overwhelming, these resolutions communicate faith in humanity and the universe. Such sympathy underlies even his most villainous characters, and our embracing of them testifies to the genius of their creator.

William Shakespeare died on April 23, 1616, the anniversary, according to tradition, of his birth fifty-three years earlier. Over his grave in Stratford Church are these words:

> Good friend for Jesus' sake forbear
> To dig the dust enclosed here.
> Blessed be the man that spares these stones,
> And cursed be he that moves these bones.

An even more famous tribute was offered by Shakespeare's contemporary, the eminent poet and playwright Ben Jonson:

> Triumph, my Britain, thou hast one to show

> To whom all scenes of Europe homage owe.
> He was not of an age, but for all time!

Indeed, Jonson's words have proven prophetic. Across the centuries and all national boundaries, Shakespeare's works have remained at the forefront, and only the Bible has been translated into more languages. The plays have been produced in virtually every society, and each audience, whether Western or Eastern, agrarian or industrialized, finds its own themes and values in them.

Nonetheless, the texts have not always been treated reverently. From 1642 through the early 1660s, when the Puritans ruled England, theaters were shut. But when the English monarchy was restored and theaters were reopened, new technical facilities were developed. More elaborate lighting and moveable scenery allowed for all sorts of realistic as well as pyrotechnical effects. Women were at last allowed to take to the stage, and thus the convention of young males in female parts disappeared.

At the same time, many scripts, including those of Shakespeare, were subject to ruthless revision that suited the tastes of the era. The most notorious rewriting was Nahum Tate's 1681 version of *King Lear*. In the eighteenth century, texts were subject to less abuse, and acting became we might call more realistic or natural. Still, satisfying audience taste remained the primary motivation, and even the supreme actor David Garrick tried his hand at rewriting *Romeo and Juliet* by creating a version in which the title characters are reunited before their deaths.

Despite such abuse, Shakespeare continues to thrive. For actors and directors, the plays remain the supreme test of skill and imagination and encourage inexhaustible approaches to production. In an attempt to achieve authenticity, contemporary companies have reverted to all-male presentations, joined recently by all-female ones. In virtually every state in our country, and in virtually every country around the world, Shakespeare festivals abound. No other dramatist receives a modicum of such attention.

Over the centuries, stories from the plays have been transformed into countless adaptations and retellings, including films, operas, symphonic portraits, ballets, and musical comedies, as well as stage productions that are veritable riffs off the formal script. Thanks to video recordings, performances that once might have disappeared forever are now available at the touch of a computer screen.

Countless eloquent and insightful lines from his plays and poetry are now an indelible part of world culture. In any book of famous quotations, samples from even the most eminent authors cover no more than a few pages. Inevitably the two largest sections, often set apart from the rest of the compilation, are devoted to the Bible and Shakespeare, with thousands of citations from each.

The popularity and influence of Shakespeare's work has inevitably given rise to critical analysis, and the staggering volume of material grows exponentially every year. No writer has been the subject of such intense study, and the multitude of critical perspectives testifies to the richness of the material, even as they reveal the critics' prejudices and limitations.

Earliest commentators focused on Shakespeare as a natural genius, whose lack of formal training led to tendencies in plot structure and character that violated long-standing "rules" of dramaturgy. By the end of the eighteenth century, concern moved away from the dictates of formality to what was to become the object of scrutiny for the next century: Shakespeare's profound understanding of humanity. The poet Samuel Taylor Coleridge emphasized that although Shakespeare deviated from the classical unities of time, place, and action, his plays held together because of unity of feeling.

During the past century, preoccupations of our era have been mirrored in attitudes toward art, and the plays of Shakespeare have been examined as closely as any works in any form. Schools of criticism now conjecture whether a single "reading" of a play is even possible or whether all interpretation is dependent on the nature and response of the audience, as well as the social, political, and economic environment in which the play is experienced.

With acknowledgment of such trends, we shall forge ahead, buttressed by two thoughts that are helpful to pose before a class begins to read anything by Shakespeare. One is best expressed by holding up a volume of the collected plays and announcing that this book is the greatest that any one person has ever written. The other is quoted by James Joyce in *Ulysses*, citing the words of Alexandre Dumas, père: "After God, Shakespeare created the most."

A Few Words About the Comedies

Shakespeare's comedies may offer the most congenial path into his plays. After all, the word *comedy* suggests at least the possibility of laughter. Still, teaching any work that is supposed to be funny is a challenge, so before starting one of Shakespeare's comedies—in fact, before studying any comic play by anyone—consider a few introductory thoughts like the ones that follow.

In all successful comic drama, characters regard themselves seriously, and much of our pleasure comes from watching them struggle to maintain dignity amid circumstances that conspire to steal that dignity. (At any time during this discussion, soliciting examples from film, television, and theater is bound to spark response.) The crucial quality is tone, and at this point two terms need to be clarified: *farce* and *comedy*. Sometimes *comedy* covers anything intended to provoke fun, and you may end up using it that way, but here you want to be precise. Most students will have heard these words, but distinguishing between them is not easy.

The essence of farce is that the audience does not take the characters seriously. Whatever emotional or physical pain they endure, we understand that it is temporary, and therefore we don't bother pondering their hopes and dreams or questioning their motivations. Instead, we watch them scrambling, slamming doors, and indulging in all sorts of silliness. For examples, point to the Marx Brothers or Abbott and Costello, but if these names are unfamiliar (the Three Stooges might still work), students will easily provide their own.

In contrast to farce is comedy, a form in which laughter is accompanied by sensibility. We may smile at the characters' foolishness, but we also realize that were the writer so inclined, the crisis at hand could resolve unhappily. Whatever the stakes, the dramatic situation touches us. For examples, suggest plays of Neil Simon, such as *The Odd Couple* or *The Sunshine*

Boys; movies like *Annie Hall* or *When Harry Met Sally*; or television shows like *M*A*S*H* or *Cheers*.

All these works date from years back, but no doubt the class will offer more recent examples. When they do, then classify each as comedy or farce, try asking, "How deeply do you care about the characters?" or, "Do you care about them at all?" You might complete this part of the discussion by noting that some high comedies have farcical elements. Yet even in cases of overlap, we can distinguish between the two forms.

A last general point about comic drama: Rarely does it last beyond one generation because so much of what makes us laugh belongs to a specific time or place. The result is that most of what amused our parents or grandparents, never mind audiences from centuries ago, seems stale today. Countless works of tragedy have endured, but only a few comic pieces from the past remain entertaining. One reason is that tragedy exalts the human dilemma, while farce and comedy, with a few exceptions, belittle it.

Which brings us to Shakespeare. His comic works still make us laugh, but we also worry about the characters and their troubles. The plays provide plenty of farcical behavior, as well as dazzling verbal humor, but beneath the fun lies sympathy for human aspiration and feeling. This balance between comic perspective and tragic awareness is the cornerstone of Shakespearean comedy.

Its pervasive theme is love in all its facets. A few so-called comedies are so dark that we can barely categorize them as such. Nonetheless, in every one men and women battle their own drives and emotions, trying to resist, control, or understand them. We experience love in its most spiritual sense, and we hear about love in its lustiest, most physical variety. Virtually all the comedies end with marriages that not only maintain the social and political order but also celebrate human passion.

One final point. In most of the comedies, women are at the center of the action. Given the social constraints of Shakespeare's age, young females had to make marriage and family their priority. Therefore we should not be surprised that they are depicted as understanding love far better than their male counterparts. What may be more surprising is that the men in the comedies are generally unfeeling or unthinking. Indeed, so admirable are the women that few seem to end up with men of comparable worth.

With these thoughts as a foundation for discussion, the class is ready to take on specific plays.

Chapter One

The Taming of the Shrew

Here is one of Shakespeare's most frequently produced works but also one of his most controversial. Students will quickly become immersed in the story, which is guaranteed to elicit passionate discussion about relationships between men and women. How do we evaluate the bond that Petruchio and Katherine establish? That question is the most intense surrounding the play.

The plot is one of the two archetypal love stories of Western culture. The first involves strangers who see each other across a crowded room or some other familiar setting, quickly fall in love, and then struggle against forces around them (or within themselves) to find happiness. The best example is *Romeo and Juliet*, and even students who have not read it will know the basic plot. They will also be able to point to countless similar versions.

The other paradigm presents two people who meet in enmity but end up in love. Even when the outcome is predictable, audiences relish seeing barriers of antagonism fall and the individuals finally acknowledge what we have known all along: that they belong together. *The Taming of the Shrew* is the classic example of the form, but, again, students will offer many more.

You might explain, too, that critics who dislike this play usually do so on one of two grounds. The first is that it is pure farce and not worth taking seriously. Indeed, many productions emphasize horseplay like hitting, slapping, shoving, and tickling, all performed at a high decibel. The second reason is exactly the opposite: that the play does have a substantial point but a dangerous one, which is to glorify the suppression of an independent, outspoken woman. You may also want to assert that the two protagonists achieve a relationship that is both subtle and easily misunderstood.

The Induction might seem extraneous, but it raises important thematic issues. After the drunken tinker, Christopher Sly, falls asleep, patrons of the tavern dress him in finery and prepare to treat him as if he is royalty:

> Persuade him that he hath been lunatic,
> And when he says he is, say that he dreams,
> For he is nothing but a mighty lord. (Induction, 1, 66–68)

One hunter sums up the prank: "He is no less than what we say he is" (Induction, 1, 74). The lord also solicits a familiar troop of players to stage a play in front of Sly, while a page will be disguised as his supposed wife, who after seven years is "overjoyed / To see her noble lord restored to health" (Induction, 1, 125–26).

Later, Sly awakens and soon is indeed convinced that he is a nobleman long under the delusion that he is a beggar:

> Am I a lord, and have I such a lady?
> Or do I dream? Or have I dreamed till now?
> I do not sleep: I see, I hear, I speak,
> I smell sweet savors, and I feel soft things. (Induction, 2, 68–71)

The entire episode suggests that the human personality is determined as much by how people treat us as by what we intrinsically are. This theme is the crux of the play to follow, and it is ostensibly performed in front of Sly. That we never see him again suggests that Shakespeare lost interest in the concept, and therefore many modern productions omit the Induction.

We next meet Lucentio, visiting Padua with the intention of following nothing but academic pursuits, as he explains to his servant:

> And therefore, Tranio, for the time I study
> Virtue, and that part of philosophy
> Will I apply that treats of happiness
> By virtue specially to be achieved. (1, 1, 17–20)

Tranio warns him that so absolute a resolution is unrealistic: "No profit grows where is no pleasure ta'en" (1, 1, 39). In the true tradition of comedy, however, Lucentio's vow shatters when Baptista and his daughters enter, along with suitors Gremio and Hortensio. The last two are entranced by Bianca, clearly her father's favorite, but tension is established quickly when Baptista explains she is not permitted to marry until her older sister does (1, 1, 50–54).

Katherine, however, remains dismayed by her prospects: "I pray you, sir, is it your will / To make a stale of me amongst these mates?" (1, 1, 57–58). She resents her father's authority, despises the men around her, and sees no hope for the future. The citizens of Padua criticize her ill nature, but we soon recognize that she is smart and witty and that the men of this town are no match for her. In Hortensio's words, "From all such devils, good Lord, deliver us!" (1, 1, 67). Thus they characterize her as a shrew, an attitude that reinforces her behavior, which in turn becomes even more disagreeable and inspires even more disapproval.

Nonetheless, Katherine seeks a suitable mate, so we are already waiting for him to appear. First, however, Lucentio admits that he, too, longs for Bianca: "But in the other's silence do I see / Maid's mild behavior and sobriety" (1, 1, 71–72). Bianca seems to confirm Lucentio's impression, as she explains to her father: "My books and instruments shall be my company, / On them to look and practice by myself" (1, 1, 83–84). Bianca pretends to be demure, but we sense that underneath her virtuous veneer lurks a hypocrite, and one component of this play is the gradual revelation of Bianca's character.

Meanwhile, what Lucentio needs is a chance to meet her, which Baptista soon provides: "Schoolmasters will I keep within my house / Fit to instruct her youth" (1, 1, 96–97). He invites Hortensio and Gremio to suggest prospects, but they are more concerned with finding a spouse for Katherine, a seemingly impossible task (1, 1, 121–41). Gremio, by the way, is a befuddled older man, a character familiar from Italian comedy.

Lucentio is another stereotype, the courtly lover, as he reveals in his overblown poetry: "Tranio, I saw her coral lips to move, / And with her breath she did perfume the air" (1, 1, 176–77). Lucentio resolves to pass himself off as Cambio, a schoolmaster, while Tranio will pretend to be Lucentio (1, 1, 208–14). The two swap clothes, but when Biondello arrives, Lucentio is forced to tell more elaborate lies about his need to conceal his identity. In contrast to all this subterfuge, the attitudes of Katherine and Petruchio will shine.

The latter enters in scene 2, and as he batters his servant, Grumio, our initial impression is that he is hypermasculine and one-dimensional. Certain lines, however, hint at something deeper:

> Antonio, my father, is deceased,
> And I have thrust myself into this maze,
> Happily to wive and thrive, as best I may. (1, 2, 55–57)

In his own way, Petruchio may be as unhappy as Katherine. This impression is reinforced when Hortensio insists that Katherine is "curst" (1, 2, 90), a threat Petruchio initially ignores: "Hortensio, peace. Thou know'st not gold's effect" (1, 2, 94). In fact, the more he hears about her, the more determined he becomes to meet her: "For I will board her, though she chide as loud / As thunder when the clouds in autumn crack" (2, 2, 96–97).

Grumio thinks his master is more than up to the challenge (1, 2, 108–17), but in return for introducing Petruchio to the family, Hortensio asks a favor of his own: that Petruchio present him to Baptista as a teacher of music (1, 2, 135–38). Before Petruchio can answer, however, the pair is joined by Lucentio, now disguised as Cambio, and Gremio. While the latter assumes that bringing Cambio to Baptista will help Gremio's own cause with Bianca (1, 2, 166–72), we enjoy the irony of Gremio's unintentionally helping a rival.

When these plotters learn that Petruchio will actually woo Katherine, they flutter in astonishment, but he dismisses them: "Think you a little din can daunt mine ears?" (1, 2, 202). The rest of the speech reflects a man whose life needs a spark. He also has little patience with these timid souls, and the realization that Katherine so frightens them clearly piques Petruchio's interest. Thus although the two seem unsuitable, they are in fact a natural couple. They just have to realize as much.

At this juncture, you might detour from the play itself, for in claiming that all he seeks from a wife is money, Petruchio says, "I come to wive it wealthily in Padua; / If wealthily, then happily in Padua" (1, 2, 76–77). Not only do we suspect that a character who claims to be interested only in money will find something else, but also these lines open one of the most popular songs in Cole Porter's musical *Kiss Me Kate*, based on *The Taming of the Shrew*. Playing this selection for the class, along with perhaps "Where Is the Life That Late I Led?" and especially "Brush Up Your Shakespeare," is bound to be helpful.

In the final lines of act 1, Bianca's suitors proudly declare their intentions, but Tranio clarifies that before any of them can win her, all must support Petruchio in his quest to win Katherine or, in Tranio's phrase, "break the ice" (1, 2, 273). Petruchio does not answer, but surely knows that he does not need help from these wimps. Meanwhile we look forward to seeing the initial encounter between the two most dynamic figures onstage.

Their mutual unhappiness is developed in the next act. First Katherine takes out her frustration by assaulting a bound Bianca, who attracts men by the bushel but refuses to commit to one: "Believe me, sister, of all the men alive / I never yet beheld that special face" (2, 1, 10–11). She prefers to dangle them all, so again we wonder, Who is the real shrew? When Baptista frees Bianca's hands, Katherine wails bitterly:

> She is your treasure, she must have a husband,
> I must dance barefoot on her wedding day
> And, for your love to her, lead apes in hell. (2, 1, 35–37)

Such was the traditional fate of old maids. Katherine's rage reflects her unhappiness, just as Petruchio's cynicism reflects his.

Now Petruchio enters with the other suitors, but unlike them he states his case directly, courting Katherine through Baptista:

> I am a gentleman of Verona, sir,
> That hearing of her beauty and her wit,
> Her affability and bashful modesty,
> Her wondrous qualities and mild behavior,
> Am bold to show myself a forward guest
> Within your house. (2, 1, 50–55)

One irony will be that such extravagant praise proves true. For the moment, however, Baptista hesitates to accept Petruchio's suit but is momentarily distracted by Hortensio and Lucentio, who enter the house as Bianca's tutors.

Then Petruchio gets down to business, literally, as he asks Baptista: "Then tell me, if I get your daughter's love, / What dowry shall I have with her to wife?" (2, 1, 126–27). Such bargaining may be distasteful to modern audiences, but it was standard Elizabethan form. After Baptista states the terms, and Petruchio orders the papers drawn, Baptista tries to put a glow on the engagement: "Ay, when the special thing is well obtained, / That is, her love, for that is all in all" (2, 1, 135–36).

We nonetheless sense that he regards his daughter as property, but when Hortensio, masquerading as a music teacher, rushes in to relate how Katherine broke a lute over his head, Petruchio is more intrigued than ever:

> Now, by the world, it is a lusty wench.
> I love her ten times more than ere I did.
> O, how I long to have some chat with her! (2, 1, 168–70)

Although he may be oblivious to his feelings, with every report about this woman she becomes more enticing.

Such discussion leads to the high point of the play, the initial meeting between Katherine and Petruchio. Before she appears, however, Petruchio explains his strategy:

> Say that she rail, why then I'll tell her plain
> She sings as sweetly as a nightingale.
> Say that she frown, I'll say she looks as clear
> As morning roses newly washed with dew. (2, 1, 178–81)

Petruchio imagines that he will win Katherine with romantic images (2, 1, 177–88), but before long he will believe those sentiments. Here the class might consider the concept of dramatic irony, wherein the audience understands what the characters do not as yet know.

The courtship scene permits all sorts of imaginative staging, as the two assault each other in various ways. Whatever the specific blocking (or movement), Petruchio's aim is to disconcert her, both verbally and physically. First he repeatedly calls her Kate, rather than the more formal Katherine she prefers. Next he resorts to lewd jokes, but she returns the badinage, which builds to genuinely racy remarks: "What, with my tongue in your tail?" (2, 1, 231). For roughly thirty-five lines, they prove themselves comic equals. At that point she strikes him, more to inflict insult than injury, but he impresses us by resisting violent retaliation and instead cautioning her, then resuming his banter.

Gradually, though, the tone shifts. As Petruchio grows aware of his delight with Katherine, he continues "taming" not just for money but also for her wit and spirit, until at last his "wooing" becomes more poetic:

> O sland'rous world! Kate like the hazel twig
> Is straight, and slender, and as brown in hue
> As hazelnuts, and sweeter than the kernels. (2, 1, 268–70)

Whether Kate fights back during this tribute or accepts it passively, we may assume that she has never heard any man speak to her so eloquently: "Where did you study all this goodly speech?" (2, 1, 277). Something about Petruchio touches her. He is, quite simply, different from any man she has ever met, and both of them understand that truth.

She is not, however, ready to surrender the personality she has cultivated, so when he tells the returning men his plan to marry her, she protests: "I'll see thee hanged on Sunday first" (2, 1, 316). Nonetheless, Petruchio proclaims their mutual devotion: "If she and I be pleased, what's that to you?" (2, 1, 322). The speech that follows may infuriate Katherine, but we can also imagine her gratified that for once a man speaks of her as his ally:

> She hung about my neck, and kiss on kiss
> She vied so fast, protesting oath on oath,
> That in a twink she won me to her love. (2, 1, 327–29)

How can she not be a little taken with him?

To facilitate discussion, consider showing the class this scene from one of the many productions of *The Taming of the Shrew* available for viewing. In addition, inform students about *Kiss Me, Petruchio*, an hour-long, two-part video on YouTube that stars Meryl Streep and the late Raul Julia. Featuring excerpts from a wonderful 1979 production in New York City's Central Park, it runs about an hour and includes the actors discussing both their individual parts and the play as a whole. The extended presentation of the courtship scene is especially enjoyable.

The next episodes contrast the compelling story of Katherine and Petruchio with the antics of the subplot. Baptista dickers with Tranio, still disguised as Lucentio, and Gremio, as the two bid to buy Bianca from him. The scene reminds us that although Petruchio may have insisted that money is his only aim, Baptista in fact treats his daughters like merchandise:

> 'Tis deeds must win the prize, and he of both
> That can assure my daughter greatest dower
> Shall have my Bianca's love. (2, 1, 362–64)

The more we see of him and the others, the more sympathetic we are to Katherine.

Meanwhile the atmosphere is thick with mistrust, especially when Baptista inquires how his daughter will thrive after her husband's death. Tranio observes that as the younger man, he will likely survive longer, but Gremio suggests that younger men, too, may die (2, 1, 412–13). Love is hardly in the air, especially when Baptista decides in favor of Tranio, then threatens to withdraw permission if Tranio's father does not provide sufficient funds (2, 1, 419–20). Left alone, Tranio vows to take the necessary steps.

In 3, 1, Hortensio and Lucentio, still pretending to be tutors, try to stake out their territory. Meanwhile Bianca manipulates the men, talking to one and whispering to the other, but Lucentio and Hortensio remain too involved in their own role-playing to recognize her game. For our part, as she alternately flatters one, then the other, we assume that whichever suitor wins will have his hands full.

On the other hand, while Petruchio delays arrival for his wedding, Katherine's outrage (3, 2, 8–20) intimates that, despite her fury at being betrothed to a "frantic fool" (3, 2, 12), she wants the ceremony to be a celebration. Inside her is a secret romantic. But keeping her off-balance is part of Petruchio's strategy, as is his bizarre apparel, described by Biondello (3, 2, 42–70). When Petruchio does appear, he brims with love and scoffs at the attention paid to his outlandish clothing: "To me she's married, not unto my clothes" (3, 2, 119). Only Tranio understands the point: "He hath some meaning in his mad attire" (3, 2, 126).

We see none of the wedding ceremony, but the description by Gremio suggests that Petruchio participated with manic enthusiasm (3, 2, 159–85). We, of course, grasp his intention: to teach Katherine that what other people think about appearance or behavior should not matter, that his love should be her only concern. She, however, does not absorb that lesson until later.

After the ceremony, everyone hopes that the couple will stay for the wedding banquet, even Katherine: "Let me entreat you" (3, 2, 204), but Petruchio refuses all supplication and insists they leave at once (3, 2, 192–99). Even so, she refuses to be whisked away without proper decorum (3, 2, 213–20), repeating *I* so often that we realize that she is trying to maintain her prerogatives.

Petruchio's response, though, is sure to elicit audience reaction. Demanding that she accompany him, he announces:

> I will be master of what is mine own.
> She is my goods, my chattels; she is my house,
> My household stuff, my field, my barn,
> My horse, my ox, my ass, my anything. (3, 2, 235–38)

By depriving her of rights and dignity, Petruchio forces her to abandon all previous patterns of behavior. Make sure, however, to note the lines that follow:

> And here she stands, touch her whoever dare.
> I'll bring mine action on the proudest he
> That stops my way in Padua. (3, 2, 239–41)

He thereby proclaims that he will protect her, and such authority must impress Katherine. Maintaining balance between these two intentions is part of the intriguing nature of this scene and of the play in general.

This moment also allows discussion of how the action should be blocked. If Petruchio tosses Katherine about and ignores her discomfort, we will be offended more than by the dialogue. But if he embraces her even as she fights to escape, the scene will communicate a different sentiment. We could make that judgment about the entire play, particularly later, when Petruchio's mistreatment of Katherine might be either playful or painful.

After the scene moves to Petruchio's home, the question of punishment becomes more acute. When Grumio recounts the humiliation that Katherine has endured on the trip (4, 1, 67–78), Curtis grasps his master's strategy: "By this reck'ning, he is more shrew than she" (4, 1, 79). And when Petruchio bullies his servants and throws away food Katherine desires, Curtis again recognizes the impetus for Petruchio's attitude: "He kills her in her own humor" (4, 1, 180). Curtis later observes that Katherine "Knows not which way to stand, to look, to speak, / And sits as one new-risen from a dream" (4, 1, 185–86), an echo of Christopher Sly (Induction, 2, 68–73).

Petruchio's address that follows is his only soliloquy, and it offers opportunity for discussion about how harsh he intends to be:

> Thus have I politicly begun my reign,
> And 'tis my hope to end successfully.
> My falcon now is sharp and passing empty,
> And, till she stoop, she must not be full-gorged. (4, 1, 188–91)

His animalistic terminology may infuriate some, but he adds, "Ay, and amid this hurly I intend / That all is done in reverend care of her" (4, 1, 203–4). How does the class imagine he says these lines? How brutal does his treatment become? Is this behavior modification excessive? Or do his tactics allow Katherine's hidden side to emerge? Is he imposing conformity on her? Or is he drawing her out? Is he cruel or benign?

As the scenes alternate between Padua and Petruchio's home, the disparity between the couples increases. Hortensio agrees to marry a rich widow (4, 2, 35–42), a tactic that Petruchio only posed. Meanwhile, Tranio persuades Biondello to play Vincentio, Lucentio's father (4, 2, 110–14). As the fraudulence in Padua grows more elaborate, Petruchio and Katherine gradually remove their own masks.

Such is the case especially when Katherine confides to Gremio her confusion about Petruchio's shenanigans: "And that which spites me more than all these wants, / He does it under name of perfect love" (4, 3, 11–12). Yet the effect of his treatment is apparent once Petruchio threatens to remove the meager food with which she is supplied, until she expresses appreciation for the repast (4, 3, 49).

Even when Katherine approves the dress the tailor created on special order (4, 3, 106–8), Petruchio destroys it, but at his command for Hortensio to reimburse the tailor (4, 3, 169), we realize that the entire sequence was a charade. Petruchio is determined not only to teach the values of amenities but also, as the couple returns to Padua, to reinforce that she should judge by quality, not appearance:

> Our purses shall be proud, our garments poor,
> For 'tis the mind that makes the body rich,
> And as the sun breaks through the darkest clouds,
> So honor peereth in the meanest habit. (4, 3, 177–80)

These lines emerge from a man who earlier spoke with apparent seriousness about his desire to marry for nothing but money. Thus in helping Katherine discover a new self, Petruchio has also brought out different aspects of his own character. The man who utters these lines is a fellow of substance, and the woman who eventually follows his advice recognizes him as such.

Before their relationship blossoms further we move back to Padua, where Baptista, deceived by the false Vincentio, gives Bianca to Tranio, thinking him Lucentio:

> Right true it is your son Lucentio here
> Doth love my daughter, and she loveth him,
> Or both dissemble deeply their affections. (4, 4, 41–43)

In fact, both are dissembling, but Baptista is so busy securing his financial future that he sends the real Lucentio, still as Cambio, to deliver marriage plans to Bianca (4, 4, 63–67). Lucentio, of course, has his own ideas and schemes with Biondello to take bride and contract and carry out a secret ceremony.

This growing understanding between Katherine and Petruchio is manifest in 4, 5, when on the road back to Padua Petruchio vacillates over whether their direction is lit by the sun or the moon. Whatever Katherine says, he shifts opinions until finally she capitulates:

> Then God be blest, it is the blessèd sun.
> But sun it is not, when you say it is not,
> And the moon changes even as your mind.
> What you will have it named, even that it is,
> And so it shall be so for Katherine. (4, 5, 21–25)

In which tone does she speak these lines? Has she been beaten into submission, and has her will been crushed? Or does she say them with a smile, acknowledging that to join Petruchio is more enjoyable than to fight him?

The answer becomes apparent a few lines later, when the arrival of old Vincentio, Lucentio's real father, inspires these lines from Petruchio: "Tell me, sweet Kate, and tell me truly, too, / Hast thou beheld a fresher gentlewoman?" (4, 5, 32–33). Hortensio fears that this outlandish remark will incite a fresh tantrum from Katherine (4, 5, 39–40), but her response surprises all three men: "Young budding virgin, fair and fresh and sweet, / Whither away, or where is thy abode?" (4, 5, 41–42).

We can imagine Petruchio's puzzlement: "Why, how now, Kate? I hope thou art not mad!" (4, 5, 46), but her response reveals her mischievous side as she takes his game one step further:

> Pardon, old father, my mistaking eyes
> That have been so bedazzled with the sun
> That everything I look on seemeth green. (4, 5, 49–51)

Both have learned the fun of playing together, and from this moment on they will be a couple not only in name but also in spirit. Again, some students will insist that Kate's personality has been crushed, but others will decide that her real personality has finally come to light, along with the realization that whoever gives the most receives the most. Note, too, how Katherine says that her judgment was hampered by the sun (4, 5, 50), a playful echo of Petruchio's earlier claim.

In act 5, all plots unite, and as individuals confront those they are pretending to be, Petruchio and Katherine stand aside to observe the chaos (5, 1, 62–63). It is embodied in one stage direction: "*Biondello, Tranio, and Merchant exit as fast as may be*" (5, 1, 112). After Lucentio's explanation (5, 1, 127–33), antagonisms cool, although the two fathers remain feeling slighted (5, 1, 136–39). This confusion is contrasted with the behavior of Katherine and Petruchio (5, 1, 145–56). She is embarrassed to kiss him in public, but after his mock threat to return home, she happily consents.

The closing scene has several important moments. First Hortensio's wife refers to Katherine as a shrew (5, 2, 29), but Katherine speaks right up, as Petruchio cheers her on (5, 2, 35, 37). Thus he has not eradicated her vitality; he merely redirected it. The three wives then leave, only to be recalled as part of a contest. Katherine wins Petruchio's bet by answering his summons first, then at his bidding explains to the other women their matrimonial duties.

Critics who cannot abide this play point directly to this speech, especially the most controversial line: "Thy husband is thy lord, thy life, thy keeper, / Thy head, thy sovereign" (5, 2, 162–63). The next section, though, is equally important:

> one that cares for thee,
> And for thy maintenance commits his body
> To painful labor both by sea and land,
> To watch the night in storms, the day in cold,
> While thou liest warm at home, secure and safe. (5, 2, 163–67)

Her meaning is clear: A husband owes his wife his very being. Katherine thus advocates what in Shakespeare's time would be considered equilibrium between the two.

She explains that such mutual responsibility parallels the bond between prince and subject (5, 2, 171), insinuating that just as a society's health is based on hierarchical structure, so happiness in a marriage is tied to order. Nonetheless, whatever the underlying theme, these days the speech is almost always performed in a manner that implies we cannot accept Katherine's words at face value.

Yet balance and proportion was an ideal of Shakespeare's age, and that ideal is one Katherine advocates. In our time, social mores are far different from those of the Renaissance, and by our standards the resolution of the play may seem chauvinistic, but for his era Shakespeare, in this play and many others, shows profound respect for the contribution of women to a society's moral and emotional health.

Some students will forever disapprove of the relationship between Petruchio and Katherine, and no matter what rationale is proposed, will find his abuse of her inexcusable. In that case, the best response is probably to suggest that on the couple's own terms, at least, they achieve a love that surpasses any in their world. Furthermore, the play itself offers a winning theatrical spectacle, as well as two characters whose vibrancy makes them among Shakespeare's most successful creations.

Chapter Two

A Midsummer Night's Dream

No play of Shakespeare's better embodies his comic mastery than this one. The plot weaves four stories fluidly. The characters are drawn from all levels of life and are alternately laughable and sympathetic. Most importantly, the language allows magic and marriage to harmonize eloquently. Indeed, this play is perhaps Shakespeare's most musical, and the class deserves to hear some of Mendelssohn's incidental music for *A Midsummer Night's Dream*, which the composer began, you should note, when he was just seventeen. Playing the introduction and the familiar "Wedding March" will surely enhance the text.

The class should also be aware that this play presents several themes that pervade Shakespeare's comedies. We see the power of imagination in romance, as well as parody of romantic convention. We see women suffering at the hands of men who are foolish, insensitive, and even brutal. We see the self-deception to which people in love are vulnerable and the potential tragedy underlying comic complications about love. And we see marriage as a celebration of the cycle of fertility and the affirmation of life.

Many of these motifs are apparent in the opening exchange between Theseus and Hippolyta. His emphasis on the moon, with its connotations of madness and change, foreshadows the disorder and unstable affections to follow, as well as male restlessness and eagerness. Meanwhile, her use of *dream* and *time* reflects the controlled romanticism typical of Shakespeare's women.

With the entrance of the young lovers, complications begin. Remember that this play was written at roughly the same time as *Romeo and Juliet*, whose fundamental tensions most students will know. Here Lysander and Hermia are in love, but her father, Egeus, prefers Demetrius as a husband for his daughter. The romantic gestures by Lysander that Egeus describes (1, 1,

27–39) are blandly stereotypical, but one phrase stands out: "feigning love" (1, 1, 32). In light of Lysander's subsequent behavior, we shall recall those words.

Given conventions of the theater, we are instinctively antagonistic toward Egeus, a dictatorial father who, like other fathers in Shakespeare, ignores his daughter's feelings. We also cannot muster support for Demetrius, who relentlessly pursues a woman who does not love him. Thus we find ourselves sympathizing with Lysander, even though he hardly seems special. Meanwhile the few words Demetrius speaks are whiny, and as the scene develops, even Theseus seems to favor Lysander.

The one character who does impress us is Hermia, feisty from the start: "I would my father looked but with my eyes" (1, 1, 58). This reference is followed by Theseus's statement: "Rather your eyes must with his judgment look" (1, 1, 59). Both lines anticipate the theme of seeing, which resounds throughout the play. Characters are constantly beset by what they imagine they view but also lack insight or understanding of what they actually do see.

In addition, Hermia's being victimized by her father's heartlessness puts us on her side, especially when Theseus delineates the punishment she faces for refusing Egeus's decree: "Either to die the death or to abjure / Forever the society of men" (1, 1, 67–68). Hermia's vigorous denial (1, 1, 81–84) indicates that she will not accept either fate passively. Nevertheless, a potentially tragic outcome threatens her, and even Lysander's declaration of intention (1, 1, 101–12) provides small comfort, given that he does not praise Hermia but disparages Demetrius and glorifies himself.

After Theseus confirms his bias by escorting Egeus and Demetrius offstage, Hermia and Lysander plot a strategy. At first Lysander muses helplessly: "The course of true love never did run smooth" (1, 1, 136), but Hermia articulates the crisis: "If then true lovers have been ever crossed, / It stands as an edict in destiny" (1, 1, 152–53). This moment is another opportunity to mention *Romeo and Juliet* and the phrase "star-crossed lovers" by the Chorus (*Romeo and Juliet*, Prologue, 6).

Finally Lysander suggests escaping to his aunt's house in the woods where he used to meet Helena, hardly a tactful remark for a man claiming to be in love. Earlier he chided Demetrius for straying with that same woman (1, 1, 108–10). Now Lysander is oblivious to a dalliance of his own. Hermia, though, shows herself alert to male behavior: "By all the vows that ever men have broke" (1, 1, 178).

We share her mistrust, especially when Helena conveniently appears in anguish over her frustrated love for Demetrius (1, 1, 184–97) and Lysander blurts out his plan to escape with Hermia:

> Tomorrow night when Phoebe doth behold
> Her silver visage in the wat'ry glass,
> Decking with liquid pearl the bladed grass

(A time that lovers' flights doth still conceal),
Through Athens' gates have we devised to steal. (1, 1, 214–18)

Ask the class whether Lysander's words to Helena seem more poetic than his earlier protestations to Hermia. Moreover, what is Lysander's strategy? Why reveal their plan at all, and why make it sound so attractive to Helena?

Hermia tries to comfort Helena, recalling their shared confidences (1, 1, 219–21). Apparently the women, no matter how intense their rivalry, share a bond based on their female identity. As the two speak, we note their varying personalities. While Hermia is more of a battler, Helena is mournful and reflective. Both, however, must deal with males on whom they cannot rely.

Perhaps here is the moment to remind the group that, as noted in this book's introduction, many of Shakespeare's comedies feature pairs of young women. We may therefore assume that in his all-male company, Shakespeare had two talented boys for whom he regularly wrote crucial parts. Moreover, given the physical descriptions of the two women in this play (Hermia is described as short and dark, Helen as tall and fair), the two young males probably fit those characteristics.

Helena's subsequent soliloquy brings out two themes familiar from other Shakespeare comedies. She notes how under the certain conditions: "Things base and vile, holding no quantity, / Love can transpose to form and dignity" (1, 1, 238–39). She immediately adds, however, "Love looks not with the eyes but with the mind" (1, 1, 240). This statement proves ironic, for throughout this work sexual attraction is almost entirely irrational. And should students fail to see the relevance of this theme, ask how many have ever looked at a couple they know and commented something to the effect, "What does she *see* in him?"

Helena concludes by resolving to tell Demetrius of Hermia's and Lysander's plan in the hope that Demetrius will follow them. Yet what does she intend to accomplish? Does she expect her loyalty to inspire Demetrius's love for her: "And, for this intelligence / If I have thanks, it is a dear expense" (1, 1, 254–55). Perhaps, but matters will go in an entirely different direction.

The introduction of the Mechanicals in scene 2 brings in the third stratum of society. As they prepare to cast their script of *Pyramus and Thisbe*, a classical story of tragic young love, the intrepidity of Nick Bottom, eager to play every part, more than compensates for the diffidence of others like Flute, who is reluctant to play Thisbe: "Nay, faith, let not me play a woman. I have a beard coming" (1, 2, 45–46). The line that perhaps encapsulates the scene is Bottom's farewell warning: "Hold or cut bowstrings" (1, 2, 107). We're not sure what it means, but it sounds wonderful.

No doubt Shakespeare was having fun with the healthy egos of some of his own actors. Meanwhile the promise that they will rehearse "by moonlight" (1, 2, 98) hints that they will be part of the upcoming lunacy, and the phrase "most obscenely" (1, 2, 104) promises linguistic fun. You might even suggest that these men, especially during the subsequent performance at court, are the most surefire comedy act ever to take the stage.

In 2, 1, the introduction of the fairy world completes the levels of comedy, and from this point on we look for parallels between this magic society and the real world of the lovers, especially because in many productions the same actor portrays Theseus and Oberon, while Titania/Hippolyta is also often a dual role. Moreover, with the entrance of Puck, "that merry wanderer of the night" (2, 1, 45), and other fairies, earthbound dimensions disappear. In Puck's words: "I do wander everywhere, / Swifter than the moon's sphere" (2, 1, 6–7). This speech establishes an atmosphere of magic and wonder that brings to life the *dream* of the title.

The subsequent bickering between Oberon and Titania reveals how jealousies that afflict human men and women exist in the fairy world as well. Their marital discord has also incited natural disorder, as Titania accuses her husband:

> Therefore the winds, piping to us in vain,
> As in revenge have sucked up from the sea
> Contagious fogs, which, falling in the land,
> Hath every pelting river made so proud
> That they have overborne their continents. (2, 1, 91–95)

With only a few words, Shakespeare creates a vivid natural panorama, suggesting that love, whether among human beings or fairies, is part of the natural cycle. The object of contention between Oberon and Titania is the changeling boy (2, 1, 21–25), and Oberon's revenge at the hands of Puck reaffirms imagery of sight:

> The juice of it on sleeping eyelids laid
> Will make or man or woman madly dote
> Upon the next live creature that it sees. (2, 1, 176–78)

The fairy world next intersects with the real world when, under the eye of Oberon, Demetrius enters, followed by a heartbroken Helena, whose feelings he never hesitates to trample: "I love thee not; therefore pursue me not" (2, 1, 195). Rarely in drama do we like a man who rejects a woman that loves him, and this play is no exception. Oddly, Demetrius never connects Helena's attraction to him with his own fruitless chase of Hermia. Furthermore, throughout this scene and several to follow, denials of love by Demetrius and Lysander are more convincing than their claims of affection, as Demetrius shows soon: "For I am sick when I do look on thee" (2, 1, 219).

Helena's response has implications beyond this play. First she pleads: "And I am sick when I look not on you" (2, 1, 220). Later, speaking about women, she says:

> Your wrongs do set a scandal on my sex.
> We cannot fight for love as men may do.
> We should be wooed and were not made to woo. (2, 1, 247–49)

Why does she find him irresistible? From what we have seen, we cannot say. Yet societal convention in Shakespeare's time forced women to remain passive in romance, forbidden to give full rein to their desires. Do such strictures exist today? Merely hinting at that possibility will guarantee response.

In these passages, by the way, Helena repeats one of the central linguistic modes of the play, as she makes a pun on "woo'd" and "woo." The words should be heard in the context of "wood," for all three sound like "wode," meaning "mad" or "frantic," and reflect the characters and their situation. Every time we hear "wood" or some version, we sense implications of "madness."

In scene 2, Oberon invades the sleeping Titania's bower to anoint her eyes with nectar: "When thou wak'st, it is thy dear. / Wake when some vile thing is near" (2, 2, 39–40). How appropriate that this prediction is followed by the entrance of Lysander and Hermia, scrambling aimlessly because Lysander has lost his way. His solution is simple: "Then by your side no bedroom me deny, / For lying so, Hermia, I do not lie" (2, 2, 57–58). The double meaning of "lie" does not escape us or Hermia, who rejects his offer: "Thy love ne'er alter till thy sweet life end!" (2, 2, 67). The irony is that as soon as he awakens, that "love" will disappear immediately.

Indeed, at that moment Helena arrives and begins to denigrate herself: "No, no, I am as ugly as a bear, / For beasts that meet me run away for fear" (2, 2, 100–101). We're not sure whether she means Demetrius, but the possibility is enough, for her self-esteem depends almost entirely on how others see her. Then Lysander awakens and begins spouting devotion to Helena:

> Who will not change a raven for a dove?
> The will of man is by his reason swayed,
> And reason says you are the worthier maid. (2, 2, 121–23)

Of course reason is utterly irrelevant.

The rest of the speech shows him preoccupied with his own self, a tendency he will never lose. What concerns Lysander are not Helena's qualities but his own desire to fall in love. Only when he speaks of the now-despised Hermia do his emotions seem legitimate: "For, as a surfeit of the sweetest things / The deepest loathing to the stomach brings" (2, 2, 144–45). The coldness of his words apparently brings Hermia out of her sleep:

> What a dream was here!
> Lysander, look how I do quake with fear.
> Methought a serpent ate my heart away,
> And you sat smiling at his cruel prey. (2, 2, 154–57)

She intuits the meanness within Lysander. The general implication is that an individual's personality, no matter what forces toy with it, inevitably emerges.

As Hermia races off in humiliation, her last line touches us: "Either death or you I'll find immediately" (2, 2, 163). We are not worried that she will die, for the fairies hold sway over everything, but her anguish hints at the potential tragedy underneath the story. Were circumstances slightly different, as in *Romeo and Juliet*, the unraveling of such a mix-up could be sad indeed.

When the Mechanicals enter to rehearse, their physical antics and linguistic fumbles are delightful, but what matters as much is their determination to be as realistic as possible, even to have someone play "Wall." The men do not trust "suspension of disbelief," an audience's willingness to accept illusion that lies at the heart of theater. In addition, human beings, especially those in love, are far more likely to believe what they want and what they dream than to accept literal truth.

When Bottom returns under Puck's spell and wearing an ass's head, in Quince's word "translated" (3, 1, 121), the others run in terror. When, however, Titania awakens and sees him, her infatuation with this creature mirrors that of the Athenian men: "So is mine eye enthrallèd to thy shape" (3, 1, 141). Bottom is less sophisticated than Lysander and Demetrius, but his response reveals greater understanding:

> Methinks, mistress, you should have little
> reason for that. And yet, to say the truth, reason
> and love keep little company together nowadays. (3, 1, 144–46)

The other men and women imagine that they control their will. Bottom has no such illusions, and thus to him Titania's adoration makes perfect sense, as do their exchanges about "wode" (madness).

In 3, 2, Oberon is pleased (at least for the moment) with Puck's account of Titania's being in love with Bottom: "My mistress with a monster is in love" (3, 2, 6), but the entrance of Demetrius and Hermia sets off a series of vituperative exchanges. She attacks him about Lysander:

> O, once tell true! Tell true, even for my sake!
> Durst thou have looked upon him, being awake?
> And hast thou killed him sleeping? O brave touch! (3, 2, 70–72)

Then she rushes off, while Demetrius demonstrates his vigor by falling asleep.

Now Oberon and Puck realize that Puck applied the magic juice to the wrong man, but almost immediately Helena enters, scorning Lysander, whose claims of love sound characteristically hollow: "Look, when I vow, I weep; and vows so born, / In their nativity all truth appears" (3, 2, 126–27). We also enjoy the irony of such comments as: "I had no judgment when to her I swore" (3, 2, 137).

When Demetrius awakes, also under the spell of the newly applied nectar, he flatters Helena in his own style:

> O, Helen, goddess, nymph, perfect, divine!
> To what, my love, shall I compare thine eyne?
> Crystal is muddy. O, how ripe in show
> Thy lips, those kissing cherries, tempting grow! (3, 2, 140–43)

Again, even under the potion, the men's personalities remain the same: Lysander spouts insidious wordplay, and Demetrius overblown imagery. Therefore Helena's accusations against their fundamental character (3, 2, 148–64) ring true.

The reentrance of Hermia sets off fireworks because the women, once allies, now accuse each other of treachery. Should we take such reversal as evidence that all women are inevitably forced into rivalry over men, even men like these, who are hardly prizes? Here the males revert to childishness. First, Demetrius claims to Helena, "I say I love thee more than he can do" (3, 2, 261), to which Lysander responds in kind, "I thou say so, withdraw and prove it too" (3, 2, 262). Again their expressions of antagonism are more vivid than any statements of affection.

When Hermia finds herself everyone's target, she turns her pugnaciousness against Helena: "You juggler, you cankerblossom, / You thief of love!" (3, 2, 296–97), so naturally Helena responds by accusing Hermia: "Fie, fie, you counterfeit, you puppet, you!" (3, 2, 303). In fact, that line should be directed at Lysander and Demetrius, who are as yet under spells.

The insults that draw the sharpest replies from Hermia are about her height: "How low am I? I am not yet so low / But that my nails can reach unto thine eyes" (3, 2, 312–13). Helena, however, does not hold back: "And though she be but little, she is fierce" (3, 2, 342). We can imagine Hermia rushing at Helena in fury: "'Little' again? Nothing but 'low' and 'little'?" (3, 2, 343). None of Helena's gibes, however, are as nasty as Lysander's: "Get you gone, you dwarf, / You minimus of hind'ring knotgrass made" (3, 2, 346–47).

This scene is ripe for imaginative staging that permits the actors to run wild. Given the power of Oberon and Puck and their determination to set matters straight, we know that all will resolve happily. What we must feel, though, is that the comedy reflects genuine distress. Finally, as Puck assumes multiple voices to distract the lovers, the two men violently pursue one that each imagines to be that of his rival, but eventually they tire and fall asleep. Such passivity does not speak well of their determination, but at least Puck removes the spell from Lysander. Order will soon be restored.

In act 4, Oberon observes Titania with Bottom and seems almost touched by her predicament: "Her dotage now I do begin to pity" (4, 1, 48). Is he sorry for her? Or jealous of her infatuation? Either way, once he removes the spell, she is horrified to see Bottom: "O, how mine eyes do loathe his visage now!" (4, 1, 81). Somehow the enchanted Titania was able to appreciate or "see" his inner qualities that now elude her. Finally she and Oberon achieve reconciliation in a musical interlude that befits the tone of the play.

The sight of the four lovers lying asleep inspires Theseus and Hippolyta to recall memories that embody the chaos we have witnessed. Theseus speaks of "musical confusion" (4, 1, 114), while Hippolyta adds: "I never heard / So musical a discord, such sweet thunder" (4, 1, 121–22). The imagery reflects a play in which voices mix but never so much that the clash of harmonies is painfully dissonant.

Once the lovers are awake (still unaware of the experience they have undergone), Egeus resumes both his scorn for Lysander and his eagerness to have Demetrius marry Hermia. Now, however, the former suitor is smitten with Helena. Yet even as Demetrius explains his feelings, he invokes the ugliness we have come to expect from him:

> To her, my lord,
> Was I betrothed ere I saw Hermia.
> But like a sickness did I loathe this food.
> But, as in health, come to my natural taste,
> Now I do wish it, love it, long for it,
> And will forevermore be true to it. (4, 1, 178–83)

Given what we have seen of Demetrius, we remain unimpressed with his sincerity.

As the lovers exit on their way to court, Hermia reaffirms the imagery of sight: "Methinks I see these things with parted eye, / When everything seems double" (4, 1, 196–97). But Demetrius, to our surprise, summarizes their story best:

> Are you sure
> That we are awake? It seems to me
> That yet we sleep, we dream. (4, 1, 201–3)

This comment notwithstanding, he is the only one who remains under the influence of the flower. Fortunately for all involved, his earlier detestation of Hermia has been forgotten.

Another sort of awakening is undergone by Bottom: "I have had a most rare vision" (4, 1, 214–15), perhaps the most charming moment in the play. He does not question what he cannot understand but believes in the wonder of his imagination:

> I will get Peter Quince to write a ballad of this
> dream. It shall be called "Bottom's Dream" because
> it hath no bottom; and I will sing it in the
> latter end of a play, before the Duke. (4, 2, 224–27)

And when he rejoins his companions, their mutual delight is a welcome contrast to the lovers' affectations.

With the plot resolved, act 5 is in a sense an epilogue, but it is vital nonetheless. Reflecting on the story that the four lovers told, Theseus unites thematic strands of the play: "The lunatic, the lover, and the poet / Are of imagination all compact" (5, 1, 7–8). We have seen examples of all three, but what gives Theseus's words a special irony is that at times all have appeared onstage.

One more spectacle serves as commentary: the guaranteed hilarity of the performance by the Mechanicals. It is selected by Theseus from several preposterous offerings, including: "'The battle with the Centaurs, to be sung / By an Athenian eunuch to the harp'" (5, 1, 48–49). If a video of the performance by Bottom and company is available, show it to the class because no analysis can do justice to such fun. Almost any production will work, but the 1968 Royal Shakespeare production featuring Helen Mirren and Judi Dench and a more recent Hollywood production with Kevin Kline are recommended.

As the performance begins, Theseus urges the listeners to be generous (5, 1, 95–111), but the actors' incompetence makes such a response impossible. First Quince introduces the enterprise by running his lines together: "Our true intent is. All for your delight / We are not here" (5, 1, 120–21). We also enjoy the excessive alliteration in Bottom's poetry: "Whereat, with blade, with bloody blameful blade, / He bravely broached his boiling bloody breast" (5, 1, 155–56).

Amid the foolishness, however, we find substance. For instance, after Theseus politely asks whether the lion will speak, Demetrius retorts with familiar sneering: "One lion may when many asses do" (5, 1, 162–63). We remember that he remains hypnotized, and thus his insult reflects more of him than he knows. Perhaps the most intriguing blunder is made by Bottom, enacting Pyramus, who overhears a comment by Theseus about whether Wall will speak (5, 1, 194–95). At once Bottom breaks character to explain:

> No, in truth, sir, he should not. "Deceiving
> me" is Thisbe's cue. She is to enter now, and I am
> to spy her through the wall. You shall see it will fall
> pat as I told you. (5, 1, 196–99)

As always, he moves innocently between art, or imagination, and reality.

Despite countless missteps, the tragic potential of the story is evident even in this burlesque, as Pyramus's grief over what he takes to be the corpse of Thisbe reduces the audience onstage and usually the one in the theater to silence. As Theseus comments: "This passion, and the death of a dear friend, would go near to make a man look sad" (5, 1, 303–4). Hippolyta adds: "Beshrew my heart but I pity the man" (5, 1, 305). How appropriate that the two royals, truly in love, are moved by the fate of Pyramus and Thisbe, while Lysander and Demetrius, perpetual buffoons, offer only derision. Hermia and Helena say almost nothing, for this story of unrequited love may touch them more than they care to admit.

The acting in this travesty, as indicated by the language, must be extravagantly overdone, and opportunities for bumbling and stumbling are myriad. But then during the main action of the play, the behavior of the lovers was often equally ridiculous. What emerges from both plot lines is Shakespeare's blend of sympathy and mockery for those swept up in love. Thereafter, Puck's closing statement of forgiveness reassures us about the order of the world, and we are led gracefully out of magic and back to reality.

Throughout *A Midsummer Night's Dream*, four stories of characters that are vastly different intermingle flawlessly, influencing and shaping one another. All, however, center on the complexities of affection and pride. Despite potential sadness that looms perilously close, we are entertained and touched by the universal predicament of human beings whose tangled emotions leave them both bewildered and beguiled.

Chapter Three

The Merchant of Venice

When any class reads this play, the first question is likely to be, "Is this really supposed to be a comedy?" Soon the discussion will turn to whether the work is anti-Semitic, then whether Shakespeare himself was, and before long students will head off in many directions. Indeed, simply to assign the play is a bold choice, and to produce it anywhere is bound to create controversy.

The crucial problem, of course, is Shylock, and no character of Shakespeare's has aroused such fervent debate. Onstage during only five scenes, he nevertheless dominates the proceedings. One reason the play is labeled a comedy is that Shylock, ostensibly the villain, receives what Shakespeare's audience may well have regarded as just punishment that contributes to a happy ending. The other reason is that the story concludes with multiple marriages, but more on that subject presently.

Before moving to Shylock, however, start with the opening scenes. First the title character, Antonio, establishes a melancholy note: "In sooth I know not why I am so sad" (1, 1, 1). His friends Salarino and Solanio suggest that he is worried about his ships, thus establishing a pervasive preoccupation with finance, but Antonio rejects that conjecture, as well as the assertion that he is in love. The force of his reply (1, 1, 48), always a tip-off in drama, alerts us to the possibility that he likely suffers from frustrated longing.

With the entrance of Gratiano, Lorenzo, and Bassanio, new energy takes over. Gratiano's observation that Antonio is depressed earns his friend's agreement:

> I hold the world but as the world, Gratiano,
> A stage where every man must play a part,
> And mine a sad one. (1, 1, 81–83)

Gratiano's subsequent banter, "Let me play the fool" (1, 1, 84), is amusing, yet no one appreciates Antonio's obvious unhappiness, even his supposed best friend, Bassanio, who remains absorbed with his own concerns: "To you, Antonio, / I owe the most in money and in love" (1, 1, 137–38). Here is another image of finance, and as usual in this play, money is linked to happiness.

Antonio's response is surprisingly passionate: "My purse, my person, my extremest means / Lie all unlocked to your occasions" (1, 1, 145–46). How profoundly is he attracted to Bassanio? Subsequent scenes will suggest that the yearning runs deep. Bassanio, however, appears oblivious, and instead extols the virtues of his new love, Portia. She is "richly left" (1, 1, 168) and, like the "golden fleece" (1, 1, 177), the object of many suitors. The problem is that Bassanio needs the "means" (1, 1, 180) to win her, and once again finance and love are intertwined. Antonio offers to provide funds (1, 1, 184–92) but does so without gusto.

Thus the opening scene establishes several points. Antonio is unhappy with existence itself, and Venice's populace is preoccupied with money and pleasure. Meanwhile Antonio's devotion to Bassanio is appreciated but returned only superficially. In sum, this world is not attractive, and Antonio's mood seems a direct product of his estrangement from it.

Antonio is not the sole character experiencing alienation, as Portia clarifies in the opening line of the next scene, miles away in Belmont: "By my troth, Nerissa, my little body is aweary of this great world" (1, 2, 1–2). Because her late father has decreed that she must wed whoever selects the correct one of three caskets, marriage and money are again tied. Portia's powerlessness annoys her so much that she dismisses every potential suitor, some cruelly: "God made him, and therefore let him pass for a man" (1, 2, 56–57). The only one she wants is Nerissa's choice, Bassanio: "I remember him well, and I remember him worthy of thy praise" (1, 2, 120–21). Portia's misery, like Antonio's, can be assuaged by only one man.

In 1, 3, the tone of the play changes with four words: "Three thousand ducats, well" (1, 3, 1), for Shylock's voice is unlike any we have heard. Shakespeare probably never met any Jews, who were expelled from England in 1290, although a small enclave remained living under the religious laws of the land. The only Jew of prominence during that era was Dr. Roderigo Lopez, a Portuguese physician to Queen Elizabeth who was executed on a dubious charge of treason. The most famous fictional Jew was the bloodthirsty Barrabas from Marlowe's *The Jew of Malta*, a character no doubt familiar to Shakespeare's audience.

Therefore what makes Shylock a villain is not just his different tradition but also his status as an alien. Just as Othello is apart because of his race and Malvolio in *Twelfth Night* because of his values, so Shylock is inherently an outsider. True, Shakespeare ascribes to Shylock stereotypically ugly characteristics, for as a money lender, one of the few professions in Venice open to Jews, he is greedy, puritanical, and vengeful. Yet he is also proud and acutely sensitive to bigotry that dominates what we soon realize is a morally ugly city. Part of the complication of this play is that Shylock's hatred of Venice and the city's hatred of him feed off each other.

We see this reciprocity when Shylock ponders Bassanio's request for a loan but rejects Bassanio's invitation to dinner:

> I will buy with you, sell with you, talk
> with you, walk with you, and so following; but I
> will not eat with you, drink with you, nor pray with
> you. (1, 3, 35–38)

The entrance of Antonio brings out even more resentment, primarily, as Shylock explains, because Antonio is Christian (1, 3, 42) but also because he interferes with Shylock's business: "He lends out money gratis and brings down / The rate of usance here with us in Venice" (1, 3, 44–45). Then Shylock adds a new note: "He hates our sacred nation. . . . Cursèd be my tribe / If I forgive him!" (48, 51–52). Is Shylock's hatred for Christians the reason Christians hate him? Or is he responding to their antipathy? Were he not Jewish but the same man, would he be so despised? Is such ill treatment as he describes directed at all Jews or at him alone?

Even Shylock's biblical reference fails to assuage Antonio's hostility: "The devil can cite Scripture for his purpose!" (1, 3, 107). Shylock defends himself:

> You call me misbeliever, cutthroat dog,
> And spet upon my Jewish gaberdine,
> And all for use of that which is mine own. (1, 3, 121–23)

But Antonio's antagonism is relentless: "I am as like to call thee so again, / To spet on thee again, to spurn thee, too" (1, 3, 140–41). Neither man seems to be able to exert self-control. Their mutual hatred is too strong.

Earlier Antonio revealed his detachment from Venice. Now disappointment with his own life takes the form of an attack on Shylock, another man apart. The reason their relationship is especially vitriolic may be that when they look at each other, they see an aspect of themselves. One filmed version that emphasizes this theme is directed by Jonathan Miller and stars Laurence Olivier, in which Shylock and Antonio look and dress alike.

Shylock eventually agrees to lend the money, but should the loan be forfeited, he imposes a shocking penalty:

> let the forfeit
> Be nominated for an equal pound
> Of your fair flesh, to be cut off and taken
> In what part of your body pleaseth me. (1, 3, 160–63)

The Elizabethan audience would have taken this stipulation as a sign of depravity, but we should see it more subtly. We might expect that if the loan were not repaid on time, Shylock would want double or triple the amount owed, but his hatred is too intense for such a conventional response. Moreover, Shylock cannot strike back at Antonio physically, so the mere thought of violating him in so grotesque a manner provides vicarious pleasure. Thus Shylock makes his demand not in hope of fulfilling it, but with the intention of making Antonio squirm.

One romantic strand returns in 2, 1, when the Prince of Morocco announces his desire to take his chance at the lottery for Portia. He is well-spoken and dignified but because of his race feels himself apart: "Mislike me not for my complexion" (2, 1, 1). Portia gleefully pronounces the penalty for losing:

> if you choose wrong
> Never to speak to lady afterward
> In way of marriage. Therefore be advised. (2, 1, 42–44)

Later comments about this prince will be less amiable.

In 2, 2 grosser comic elements take the stage with Shylock's servant, Lancelot Gobbo, and his blind father. The gibes from the son are more cruel than witty, but one line stands out: "It is a wise father that knows his own child" (2, 2, 74–75). We think of Portia's father condemning his daughter to be the object of the lottery, and soon Shylock shall try to control his daughter's passion.

The scene ends with Gratiano's asking to accompany Bassanio to Belmont and Bassanio's urging him to put on a sober front:

> Pray thee take pain
> To allay with some cold drops of modesty
> Thy skipping spirit. (2, 2, 187–89)

Gratiano's reply (2, 2, 192–200) suggests that he knows that he is a fraud but doesn't care. Eventually Gratiano stands for the city of Venice itself, in that he maintains a genial exterior but underneath nourishes cruelty.

In the next scene, Jessica establishes her own difficult paternal relationship but adds a qualifying note by promising to become a Christian (2, 3, 16–21). Her desperation to flout her father's authority is a familiar dramatic ploy, but here it is complicated by the religious dimension. It is also tainted by Lorenzo's plans to steal not only Jessica but also gold and jewels (2, 4, 34–36), another example of the link between love and money. Moreover, Lorenzo seems unbothered that Jessica's father is a Jew. Does her willingness to convert excuse her in his eyes? Or is the core of Venice's distaste for Shylock rooted in something other than religion?

That question becomes more complex in the next scene, when Shylock rails against the parties pervasive in Venice (2, 5, 29–40). Does he hate these revels because they are as decadent as he says? Or because he is not welcome? If Gratiano is any indication, Venice is devoted to pleasure, but is that impression fair? Both sides seem unsavory, and thus Shakespeare seems to dramatize pervasive hypocrisy.

In 2, 6, a familiar Shakespearean strategy is invoked—a girl disguising herself as a boy to escape with her lover—but here, too, the dialogue is suffused with talk of money, notably from Jessica: "I will make fast the doors and gild myself / With some more ducats, and be with you straight" (2, 6, 51–52). Even she understands that part, or maybe most, of her attention from Lorenzo is because of her father's wealth.

Back in Belmont, the Prince of Morocco reads the inscription outside the gold casket: "'Who chooseth me shall gain what many men desire.' / Why that's the lady! All the world desires her" (2, 7, 42–44). We never expected him to select the right casket, and like many suitors in Shakespeare's comedies he is deceived by the contrast between appearance and reality. Even so, Portia's comment on his leaving confirms her nasty edge: "Let all of his complexion choose me so" (2, 7, 87).

The appearance of Solanio and Salarino reflects an intriguing strategy by Shakespeare. Instead of Shylock's revealing his daughter's disappearance, these two communicate the information while simultaneously deriding his preoccupation: "'My daughter, O my ducats, O my daughter! / Fled with a Christian! O my Christian ducats!'" (2, 8, 15–16). More than ever, we feel the hatred of Venice for Shylock, and when we see him again, we expect it to be repaid in kind.

The Prince of Aragon is the next suitor to try for Portia's hand, but he lacks the dignity and decency that characterized Morocco. Thus we are not surprised when he makes what he assumes will be an unusual selection:

> I will not choose what many men desire,
> Because I will not jump with common spirits
> And rank me with the barbarous multitudes. (2, 9, 33–35)

We also expect that he will discover the wrong portrait, which turns out to be that of a fool, along with the comment: "'Who chooseth me shall have as much as he deserves'" (2, 9, 62–63). The good news for Portia is that a young Venetian has arrived with "Gifts of rich value" (2, 9, 99). Both she and Nerissa are overjoyed, and our expectations appear to be coming true, with the understanding, of course, that Bassanio brings the necessary funds.

When Salerio and Salarino open act 3 with the word that Antonio's ship has been lost, Shylock reacts with malicious glee: "To bait fish withal; if it will feed nothing else, it will feed my revenge" (3, 1, 52–53). A few lines later, his attitude seems to change into a plea that has become a paradigm for racial tolerance: "Hath not a Jew eyes?" (3, 1, 57–58). But that softening of his spirit soon turns into something more discomforting:

> If a Christian wrong
> a Jew, what should his sufferance be by Christian

> example? Why, revenge! The villainy you teach me I
> will execute, and it shall go hard but I will better the
> instruction. (3, 1, 68–72)

Is his true nature emerging, or is he simply reacting to treatment by Venice? How we answer that question goes a long way to deciding how we view the play as a whole.

A side note: Sometimes we like to believe that, when an individual survives great suffering, whether physical, spiritual, or both, such endurance ennobles that person, who will thereafter be more compassionate and tolerant of human failings. Shylock contradicts that belief, for experience has only embittered him and left him incapable of empathizing with anyone.

As we see in his conversation with his friend Tubal, when Shylock's fury overflows:

> I would my
> daughter were dead at my foot and the jewels in her
> ear; would she were hearsed at my foot and the
> ducats in her coffin. (3, 1, 87–90)

He is apparently unable to distinguish between his daughter and his money, and we sense him losing human feeling. Even the confirmation about Antonio's ship soothes him only temporarily, for Tubal also reports that Jessica has sold a precious family ring for a monkey. As the news drives Shylock deeper into madness, his insistence on literally carrying out his bond with Antonio becomes more understandable.

From this potential violence, the play turns back to romance and Bassanio's choice of the casket. Despite her obvious feelings, Portia is forbidden to aid in his decision: "I could teach you / How to choose right, but then I am forsworn" (3, 2, 10–11). Still, the song her musicians perform (3, 2, 65–74) includes several rhymes with *lead*, so perhaps we should hear a subconscious suggestion. In any case, we have no doubt he will select wisely, but his reasoning for rejecting the gold and silver caskets is telling:

> Thus ornament is but the guilèd shore
> To a most dangerous sea, the beauteous scarf
> Veiling an Indian beauty; in a word,
> The seeming truth which cunning times put on
> To entrap the wisest. (3, 2, 99–103)

In sum, Bassanio has the capacity to distinguish between reality and appearance.

How are we to regard him? He is on a quest, but whether that quest is for love or fortune is unclear. Is he willing to use Antonio's funds to further his cause? Obviously, but is Bassanio aware of the depth of his friend's affection? Does Bassanio even care about that affection? His distaste for Shylock is apparent, but again, we cannot be certain whether Bassanio scorns an irritating money lender or mirrors Antonio's hatred.

When Bassanio selects the right casket, the response between him and Portia is rapturous, but even here the language of finance intrudes:

> A thousand times more fair, ten thousand times
> More rich, that only to stand high in your account
> I might in virtues, beauties, livings, friends,
> Exceed account. (3, 2, 158–61)

Portia, in turn, gives him a ring, then articulates the perpetual doubt that Shakespeare's heroines maintain about men:

> I give them with this ring,
> Which, when you part from, lose, or give away,
> Let it presage the ruin of your love,
> And my vantage to exclaim on you. (3, 2, 175–78)

We expect that this ring will be part of the subsequent plot. When this pair is joined by Gratiano and Nerissa, unexpectedly but conveniently announcing their own engagement, then by Lorenzo and Jessica, the romantic circle is complete.

It quickly darkens, however, and naturally the concern is money. Salerio brings the letter detailing Antonio's losses, and Bassanio is forced to confess that the merchant is the source of Bassanio's capital. Jessica adds that she heard her father swear:

> That he would rather have Antonio's flesh
> Than twenty times the value of the sum
> That he did owe him. (3, 2, 298–300)

Nonetheless, Portia is convinced that extra payment will save Antonio, and again money is treated as equivalent to affection.

In the jail where Antonio awaits trial, Shylock remains implacable: "I'll have my bond. I will not hear thee speak. / I'll have my bond, and therefore speak no more" (3, 3, 13–14). We sense that the more urgently others beg him to forgo his appalling sentence, the more determined he becomes to carry it out. His hatred is turning into obsession, even at the price of financial recompense far beyond what he originally set out.

More startling is Antonio's attitude. We might expect him to try every legal recourse to overturn the sentence, but instead he surrenders fatalistically: "I'll follow him no more with bootless prayers. / He seeks my life. His reason well I know" (3, 3, 22–23). In fact, Antonio seems to have only one desire: "Pray God Bassanio come / To see me pay his debt, and then I care not" (3, 3, 38–39). He sounds eager to die, as long as he enjoys the perverse satisfaction of knowing that married Bassanio will perpetually bear the burden of Antonio's sacrifice.

Does Antonio believe that Bassanio's adoration for Portia has tainted the friendship between the two men? Is Antonio a frustrated homosexual whose unhappiness is a consequence of Bassanio's refusal to reciprocate? Perhaps Antonio is tormented by his inability to express his feelings or baffled by urges within himself that he cannot fathom. Whatever the reason, Antonio's loneliness parallels Shylock's religion.

Portia, meanwhile, has her own strategy, as well as reasons for pursuing it. She wants to help Bassanio's best friend escape punishment, but as she dons the garb of a young male lawyer, she explains another private cause:

> I have within my mind
> A thousand raw tricks of these bragging jacks
> Which I will practice. (3, 4, 79–81)

A woman who has felt herself treated like a trophy finally has opportunity to act on her own, and she intends to take full advantage.

Jessica, too, determines her path, as she explains to Lancelet: "I shall be saved by my husband. He hath made me a Christian" (3, 5, 18–19). In light of Shylock's subsequent fate, that line has serious ramifications. When Lorenzo enters, the intimation is that Jessica has escaped what she sees as her father's pernicious influence and blossomed into a self-possessed young woman. Such is the power of love, even in the dark setting of this play. Whether we are as impressed with her as she is with herself is another matter.

In the courtroom, the judge offers Shylock a chance to retract his claim, "thy strange apparent cruelty" (4, 1, 22), but Shylock's answer implies that he believes that he is answering Venice's cruelty (and the Duke's) with greater cruelty of his own:

> I have possessed your Grace of what I purpose,
> And by our holy Sabbath have I sworn
> To have the due and forfeit of my bond. (4, 1, 36–38)

Yet Shylock intuits that his mission is irrational:

> So I can give no reason, nor I will not,
> More than a lodged hate and a certain loathing
> I bear Antonio, that I follow thus
> A losing suit against him. (4, 1, 60–63)

Even the promise of triple payment does not move him. Rather, he comments on Venice's slave practice (4, 1, 90–104), reminding everyone onstage and in the audience of the city's values.

Still, those in the court clearly sympathize with Antonio, and Shylock stands alone. So, in an odd way, does Antonio, whose resignation articulated in the previous scene carries over:

> I am a tainted wether of the flock,
> Meetest for death. The weakest kind of fruit

> Drops earliest to the ground, and so let me.
> You cannot be better employed, Bassanio,
> Than to live still and write mine epitaph. (4, 1, 116–20)

Once again he ends with the thought of Bassanio's suffering over Antonio's fate, haunted by what Antonio considers to be betrayal.

The arrival of Nerissa disguised as a law clerk (Bellario) brings out the ugly side of Gratiano. Until now, he has essentially played the "fool," but at this moment his viciousness toward Shylock emerges:

> Thy currish spirit
> Governed a wolf who, hanged for human slaughter,
> Even from the gallows did his fell soul fleet. (4, 1, 135–37)

Shylock remains unmoved: "I stand here for law" (4, 1, 144). But with the entrance of Portia (as the lawyer Balthazar), we hear the most crucial question of the play: "Which is the merchant here? And which the Jew?" (4, 1, 176). Whether either man wants to believe so, both are possessed by hatred, both base their lives on monetary reward, and both are outcasts in hedonistic Venice.

Portia soon begins a speech that has come down to us as a formidable plea for compassion: "The quality of mercy is not strained" (4, 1, 190). It ends, though, with a sentence that almost invites Shylock to discharge his threat:

> I have spoke thus much
> To mitigate the justice of thy plea,
> Which, if thou follow, this strict court of Venice
> Must needs give sentence 'gainst the merchant
> there. (4, 1, 208–12)

Still, Shylock insists on his bond but with a curious phrase: "Shall I lay perjury upon my soul? / No, not for Venice!" (4, 1, 237–38). Does he mean that he would not compromise for all the wealth in Venice? Or for its people?

As Antonio's punishment looms as inevitable, he continues brooding: "Repent but you that you shall lose your friend / And he repents not that he pays your debt" (4, 1, 290–91). This confession inspires one from Bassanio: "But life itself, my wife, and all the world / Are not with me esteemed above thy life" (4, 1, 296–97). In response, Portia's and Nerissa's asides about the men's wives contribute a measure of irony, but we wonder about Portia herself. Not only is she leading Shylock on, but she also is allowing her husband and his best friend to agonize over the latter's impending death. Where is her "quality of mercy"?

With execution of sentence imminent, Portia encourages Shylock to become even more demonic (4, 1, 315–16), until she plays her trump card: "Tarry a little. There is something else" (4, 1, 318). As Gratiano taunts Shylock, Portia lays down impossible strictures, leading Shylock to ask merely for the principal he is owed (4, 1, 350). Bassanio is almost grateful: "I have it ready for thee. Here it is" (4, 1, 351), but now Portia turns into the most vengeful member of the court:

> Thou hast contrived against the very life
> Of the defendant, and thou has incurred
> The danger formerly by me rehearsed.
> Down, therefore, and beg mercy of the Duke. (4, 1, 375–78)

Whether Shylock kneels is unclear, but the Duke does display what Shakespeare's audience would have judged to be generosity. Although half of Shylock's money goes to Antonio and the other half to the state, Shylock will be permitted to live. Antonio, however, administers a more insidious punishment: only half of Shylock's money will be given to Antonio, but upon Shylock's death, the rest will go to Lorenzo and Jessica. What's more, and here is the final blow, Shylock must become a Christian.

At this point we might wonder whether the letter of the law always reflects its spirit. Can a good law be perverted for immoral ends? Or a bad law for beneficent ones? Whatever our view, Shakespeare's audience would have deemed the conditions imposed on Shylock as generous. First, Lorenzo and Jessica are romantic characters, and their reward would seem deserved. In addition, Shylock's becoming a Christian would be, as Jessica stated earlier (3, 5, 18–19), his only opportunity for salvation. But to audiences of our day, both stipulations are unquestionably intended to destroy Shylock financially as well as personally.

How Shylock says "I am content" (4, 1, 410), then his final lines, may bring a particular production into focus. The words may be whispered, or they may be muttered with restrained fury. The former choice would emphasize the character's helplessness and bring out those elements of his character that approach the tragic. Such is the tone of the Olivier production mentioned earlier, when Shylock, once offstage, emits a chilling wail. On the other hand, to utter these lines with hostility would emphasize his villainy and tilt the play toward the comic, although just how funny it ever becomes is open to question.

With tensions dissipated, we might expect Portia to drop her disguise. Instead, as yet still pretending to be Balthazar, she forces Bassanio to surrender the ring that he swore he would keep forever. Only Antonio seems unperturbed by the sacrifice:

> My Lord Bassanio, let him have the ring.
> Let his deservings and my love withal
> Be valued 'gainst your wife's commandment. (4, 1, 467–69)

Perhaps he is eager to have Portia angry with Bassanio and for Bassanio then to return his devotion to Antonio.

Portia, however, is not finished and, in the next scene whispers an aside to Nerissa:

> We shall have old swearing
> That they did give the rings away to men;
> But we'll outface them, and outswear them, too. (4, 2, 19–21)

Portia has enjoyed toying with these men and is unwilling to surrender authority even to the husband she loves. True, such games are inherent in romantic comedy, but after Portia's treatment of Shylock in court, this mischief confirms her malicious wit.

In act 5, back in Belmont and away from the contaminating influence of Venice, the presence of Shylock has been purged, and romantic elements take center stage, as Lorenzo recalls other famous lovers, then says: "How sweet the moonlight sleeps upon this bank" (5, 1, 62). Even as Jessica celebrates, though, she retains some of her father's values: "I am never merry when I hear sweet music" (5, 1, 77). But Lorenzo does not permit her to wallow:

> The man that hath no music in himself,
> Nor is not moved with concord of sweet sounds,
> Is fit for treasons, stratagems, and spoils. (5, 1, 92–94)

We know he is alluding to Shylock, but he might unintentionally be referring to Antonio.

When Portia enters, she maintains the aura of good feeling: "How far that little candle throws his beams! / So shines a good deed in a naughty world" (5, 1, 99–100). The sentiment is comforting, but as we remember her earlier campaign against Shylock, she seems not so warm. That impression is reinforced when she and Nerissa maintain the deception about the ring. Even when Gratiano and Bassanio confess that it was given to the young lawyer who saved Antonio, Portia continues to humiliate her husband. Speaking of the imaginary Balthazar, she says: "I'll not deny him anything I have, / No, not my body, nor my husband's bed" (5, 1, 243–44).

The two women even claim to have slept with Balthazar and his clerk; only then do they admit the charade. Forgiveness and love are exchanged, but the one person left outside the romantic atmosphere is Antonio, despite encouraging tidings that "my ships / Are safely come to road" (5, 1, 307–8). He has only his funds to sustain him, and they are not sufficient. Nerissa, meanwhile, has similar reassurance for Jessica: the legal decree guaranteeing that upon Shylock's death, his fortune will be left to her. To the very end, love and money are inseparable.

When all the strands of *The Merchant of Venice* are seen as a whole, the dominant quality of the play is egotism. Shylock is obsessed with money, his daughter, and his hatred of Venice. Antonio has no way to fulfill his passion for Bassanio. Portia seeks to exercise freedom. Lorenzo and Jessica are attracted to each other, but he also wants her money, and she uses him as a pass to freedom.

Even in the midst of this pervasive yen for gratification, however, Shylock towers over the play. Virtually all the themes, including the nature of the law, revolve around him. To go back to the beginning of this chapter, is the play anti-Semitic? And is the playwright? The answer to both questions is no, but the play is set in an anti-Semitic society, and the object of venom is Shylock, so he is the one who receives the bulk of the hatred. Admittedly, he is often dislikeable, and in his hunger for revenge he becomes almost maniacal. Yet whatever the character's defects, Shakespeare could not help but invest in Shylock an unquenchable dignity and humanity.

Chapter Four

Twelfth Night, or *What You Will*

The title *Twelfth Night* suggests the final days of the Christmas season, a traditional time of feasting and revelry. Accordingly, the play is filled with boisterous humor but also features several qualities familiar from Shakespearean comedy: self-involved lovers, mistaken identity (especially about gender), and a comic villain who suffers severe punishment. But the alternative title, *What You Will*, the only subtitle Shakespeare ever provided, suggests a more complex vision. Indeed, what may be regarded as Shakespeare's last romantic comedy is dominated by the abuse of "will." Thus despite much laughter, something unsettling permeates this work.

The tone is established in Orsino's opening lines:

> If music be the food of love, play on.
> Give me excess of it, that, surfeiting,
> The appetite may sicken and so die. (1, 1, 1–3)

He may seem like a stereotypical lovesick romantic, but his words *excess*, *surfeiting*, *appetite*, *sicken*, and *die* communicate ardor bordering on decadence. Orsino not does merely seek pleasure; he wallows in it. Moreover, when the music stops, his display of temper suggests a desperate need for stimulation.

His obsession is paralleled by that of the woman he loves, Olivia, who mourns her dead brother so intensely that she has cut herself off from the world (1, 1, 26–34). Yet Orsino finds this compulsion irresistible and imagines how steadfast her devotion will be when she turns to romance (1, 1, 35–43). He is unmoved by her sorrow but selfishly waits for her to make him the object of her inordinate fervor. Thus both characters yield to their wills, their capacity for self-indulgence.

In 1, 2, Viola quickly proves herself an energetic figure. Her brother, too, has apparently died (although the uncertain circumstances at sea suggest he may reappear), but when she learns of Olivia's unhappiness, Viola resolves to serve her (1, 2, 43–46). With the help of the trustworthy Captain who transports her, Viola (almost an anagram of *Olivia*) will disguise herself as man and seek a place in the court of Orsino, about whom she has conveniently heard. She even invokes Orsino's own imagery: "for I can sing / And speak to him in many sorts of music" (1, 2, 60–61), hinting that their relationship will blossom.

In 1, 3, we move from romance to gross comedy, led by the pleasure-seeking Sir Toby Belch: "I am sure care's an enemy to / life" (1, 3, 2–3). In his lust for food, drink, and other amusement, he may remind us of Falstaff (*Henry IV, Part 1*), but Falstaff's outrageous behavior is modulated by wit as well as affection. Sir Toby, however, spends Sir Andrew's three thousand ducats a year (1, 3, 22) while disparaging him as a "fool" (1, 3, 30) and a "coward" (1, 3, 31). Sir Toby also lives off his niece, Olivia, and his jocularity is laced with cruelty. Therefore as Orsino and Olivia embody the dark side of love, Sir Toby is the dark side of appetite.

The appearance of Sir Andrew Aguecheek confirms Sir Toby's view of him. From the start Sir Andrew remains oblivious to sexual innuendoes in Maria's use of *dry* (1, 3, 73) and *barren* (1, 3, 79). He is also gullible enough to accept Sir Toby's outlandish insistence that Sir Andrew as yet has a chance to win Olivia's hand in marriage: "Tut, there's life in 't, man" (1, 3, 109). Sir Andrew even agrees that he is a worthy suitor:

> I am a fellow o' th'
> strangest mind i' th' world. I delight in masques
> and revels sometimes altogether. (1, 3, 110–12)

His foolish self-delusion is vulnerable to manipulation, as Sir Toby repeatedly demonstrates.

By 1, 4, Viola (now dressed as a man and called Cesario) has already fallen in love with Orsino and asks Valentine: "Is he inconstant, sir, in his favors?" (1, 4, 6–7). She probably hopes the answer will be both yes and no, for she seeks a man who is loyal yet also wants Orsino's affections to switch to her. Meanwhile, Orsino finds himself surprised by Viola's allure:

> Diana's lip
> Is not more smooth and rubious, thy small pipe
> Is as the maiden's organ, shrill and sound,
> And all is semblative a womans part. (1, 4, 34–37)

Although Orsino assumes Cesario is a man, he is attracted to "him" as if he were a woman. We remember, of course, that Viola is being played by a man pretending to be a woman, who now pretends to be a man.

The moment raises many questions about gender and sexual orientation likely to provoke class discussion, especially if figures from film or music are mentioned. How do we define *masculine* and *feminine*? Which qualities are inherent in those labels? How do we explain the nature of sexual attraction? Why are different individuals aroused by certain physical attributes and repelled by others? These issues will recur throughout the play, especially when in Orsino's name Cesario courts Olivia.

In 1, 5 we meet Feste, identified as the Fool, who banters playfully, first with Maria, then with Olivia. Feste's jests have a melancholy streak, as he mocks even his mistress: "The more fool, madonna, to mourn for your brother's soul, being in heaven" (1, 5, 68–69). Olivia finds Feste amusing, but her steward, Malvolio, has no tolerance for wordplay nor for anyone who distracts Olivia from him: "I marvel your Ladyship takes delight in such a barren rascal" (1, 5, 81–82).

Yet no matter how sad she might be, Olivia sees through Malvolio's attitude: "O, you are sick of self-love, Malvolio, and taste with a distempered appetite" (1, 5, 89–90). Not only does Olivia judge Malvolio correctly, but her evaluation applies to several characters preoccupied with their own feelings. Malvolio may be the most guilty and thus deserves the harshest retribution, but in this play self-love is pervasive.

At this moment, Sir Toby's obnoxious interruption communicates the flavor of the environment in which Malvolio exists: "Lechery? I defy lechery" (1, 5, 124). The steward's subsequent report on the visiting Cesario suggests that he resents not only Sir Toby but any male rival: "One would think his mother's milk were scarce out of him" (1, 5, 160–61). His manner is supercilious, and he is easy to dislike, but as the play continues, our attitude toward him becomes more problematic.

Soon Cesario fulfills "his" assignment by wooing Olivia in Orsino's name:

> My lord and master loves you. O, such love
> Could be but recompensed though you were
>   crowned
> The nonpareil of beauty. (1, 5, 252–55)

Viola even captures Orsino's extravagance: "With adorations, fertile tears, / With groans that thunder love, with sighs of fire" (1, 5, 257–58). Olivia, however, is unmoved by such standard masculine fare and asks how Cesario might woo her in his own name, to which Viola replies:

> Make me a willow cabin at your gate
> And call upon my soul within the house. . . .
>   . . . O, you should not rest
> Between the elements of air and earth
> But you should pity me. (1, 5, 271–72, 277–79)

Olivia's stunned response reveals Viola's impact : "You might do much" (1, 5, 280), and almost at once Viola realizes that Olivia has abandoned interest in Orsino (1, 5, 285).

The implication of the exchange is that as a woman, Viola understands how to appeal to the sensibilities of another female, and now Olivia, taken with Cesario's capacity to offer affection, falls for "him." Here is a moment to ask the class about how in life men and women proceed along different lines of thought and often fail to intuit one another's desires or to sympathize with one another's feelings.

We understand that this relationship has no future, but immediately we meet an alternative to Viola: her twin brother, Sebastian, who believes that in fact she was the one who drowned. Sebastian, too, is headed for Orsino's court, so immediately we anticipate confusion. Meanwhile we see the obvious devotion of Antonio for Sebastian: "But come what may, I do adore thee so / That danger will seem sport, and I will go" (2, 1, 46–47). Is this generosity another variety of sexual attraction?

In 2, 2, we are brought back to Olivia's home, where Malvolio reluctantly returns a ring Cesario supposedly left. Viola understands the reality of the moment:

> My master loves her dearly,
> And I, poor monster, fond as much on him,
> And she, mistaken, seems to dote on me. (2, 2, 33–35)

She is bothered that her deception causes another woman pain, for Viola is aware of how acute a woman's sentiments may be: "How easy is it for the proper false / In women's waxen hearts to set their forms!" (2, 2, 29–30). She acknowledges how the two sides of her identity clash: "O Time, thou must untangle this, not I. / It is too hard a knot for me t' untie" (2, 2, 40–41). The situation is comic, but the emotion is genuine.

The scene brings back the raucous behavior of Sir Toby and Sir Andrew, reveling in songs performed by Feste and intended indirectly for Olivia. One dramatizes a search for love: "Your true love's coming, / That can sing both high and low" (2, 3, 41–42). The other dwells on the transience of life: "Then come kiss me, sweet and twenty. / Youth's a stuff will not endure" (2, 3, 52–53). Both themes continue to preoccupy Feste.

The celebration is cut off by Malvolio, offended by this display: "My masters, are you mad?" (2, 3, 87). We note the familiar *mad*, as well as Malvolio's plea for order: "Is there no respect of place, persons, nor time in you?" (2, 3, 92–93). Sir Toby's first reaction is to sneer: "Art any more than a steward?" (2, 2, 113–14). After all, Sir Toby is a knight and therefore Malvolio's superior. Sir Toby follows with one of the most famous lines of the play: "Dost thou think, because thou art virtuous, there shall be no more cakes and ale?" (2, 3, 114–15).

After more insults, Malvolio storms off, and Maria explains why she and the others detest him: "The devil a puritan that he is" (2, 3, 145). Their feelings should probably be ascribed to Shakespeare as well. The Puritans perpetually petitioned to have theaters shut down, and throughout Shakespeare's plays puritanical figures are disparaged. Shylock in *The Merchant of Venice* is certainly one, and if more names are needed, you may point to Cassio in *Othello*, Octavius in *Antony and Cleopatra*, Prince John in *Henry IV, Part 2*, and Angelo in *Measure for Measure*.

Yet does Malvolio deserve such hatred? Admittedly he is overbearing and humorless, but he is only carrying out Olivia's orders, and even then he must deal with Sir Toby, who is equally full of himself. All Malvolio tries to do is his job, for which he will suffer mightily. His snootiness surely requires comeuppance, but the crowd that annoys him is too unpleasant to have the right to punish anybody.

We also observe that the gimmick of sending him a letter ostensibly from Olivia originates with Maria. When she leaves, Sir Toby expresses his admiration: "She's a beagle true bred, and one that adores me" (2, 3, 177–78). Sir Andrew's reply is one of the play's most touching lines: "I was adored once, too" (2, 3, 179). As ridiculous as he can be, even Sir Andrew feels the pangs of longing.

In Orsino's court, the Duke and Cesario still commiserate over Orsino's frustrated love and the contrast he draws between men's and women's affection:

> Our fancies are more giddy and unfirm,
> More longing, wavering, sooner lost and worn,
> Than women's are (2, 4, 38–40)

The lines resound ironically, especially because Viola must stifle her love. Somehow Feste ends up singing here as well, and his lyrics maintain his reflective mood: "Come away, come away, death" (2, 4, 58).

Following an expression of such longing, Orsino's feelings overflow:

> There is no woman's sides
> Can bide the beating of so strong a passion
> As love doth give my heart. . . .
>   Make no compare
> Between that love a woman can bear me
> And that I owe Olivia. (2, 4, 103–5, 111–13)

Viola can only answer as Cesario:

> My father had a daughter loved a man
> As it might be, perhaps, were I a woman,
> I should your Lordship. (2, 4, 118–20)

She adds:

> We men may say more, swear more, but indeed
> Our shows are more than will; for still we prove
> Much in our vows but little in our love. (2, 4, 128–30)

Having accidentally mentioned her "sister," Viola faces Orsino's question: "But died thy sister of her love, my boy?" (2, 5, 131). Viola scrambles to answer: "I am all the daughters of my father's house, / And all the brothers, too" (2, 5, 132–33). The moment is ironic, the confusion laughable, the predicament moving, and the scene ingenious.

In the garden of Olivia's house, while Sir Toby and the others fulminate over Malvolio's arrogance, the object of their plot comes across the letter written by Maria. Malvolio enjoys imagining how he might put Sir Tony in his place: "'You must amend your drunkenness'" (2, 5, 73), to which Toby can barely restrain his outrage: "Out, scab!" (2, 5, 74). As Malvolio gradually deduces the apparent authorship of the letter, he unwittingly utters a series of obscenities (2, 5, 88–91), and the nature of the class will determine how these should be handled.

Finally Malvolio accepts the fiction that he is the object of Olivia's desire: "'Some are born great, some achieve greatness, and some have greatness thrust upon 'em'" (2, 5, 149–50), and he prepares to fulfill her wishes. The crucial instructions are that he should wear yellow stockings, cross-gartered, and that he should keep smiling. We anticipate the moment as much as the characters onstage do.

The encounter between Viola and Feste is winning, even after Feste hints that he can discern Viola's identity: "Now Jove, in his next commodity of hair, send thee a beard!" (3, 1, 46–47). Even Viola suspects Feste knows the truth: "This fellow is wise enough to play the Fool, / And to do that well craves a kind of wit" (3, 1, 61–62). Viola appreciates Feste's gifts but understands that his view of life leaves him outside the action. The fun for him is playing, not winning or losing.

Sir Toby and Sir Andrew then invite Viola to revisit with Olivia. After quickly disclaiming all interest in Orsino, the women exchange a succession of evocative lines (3, 1, 145–49) that reveal Olivia's hope and Viola's acknowledgment of reality, until at last Olivia can no longer contain herself:

> By maidhood, honor, truth, and everything,
> I love thee so, that, maugre all thy pride,
> Nor wit nor reason can my passion hide. (3, 1, 158–60)

Now, like Orsino, she pines for someone, but this person rejects her. She also affirms a theme familiar from numerous other comedies of Shakespeare: the conflict between reason and passion in matters of love. Viola's response reflects the same battle but from her singular perspective:

> I have one heart, one bosom, and one truth,
> And that no woman has, nor never none
> Shall mistress be of it, save I alone. (3, 1, 166–68)

She also reminds us that she is essentially alone in the world.

When in the next scene Sir Andrew confesses frustration with his failure to court Olivia, Sir Toby encourages him to challenge his new rival, Cesario, to a duel. In case we ever thought Sir Toby felt sympathy for Sir Andrew, this scene confirms the complete lack of care:

> For Andrew, if he were
> opened and you find so much blood in his liver as
> will clog the foot of a flea, I'll eat the rest of th'
> anatomy. (3, 2, 59–62)

Maria's report about Malvolio's altered appearance and manner keeps the plot whirling.

The next scene, however, reminds us that love can take another form, as Sebastian and Antonio plan strategy. Antonio pronounces his affection and loyalty:

> My willing love,
> The rather by these arguments of fear,
> Set forth in your pursuit. (3, 3, 11–13)

Such open devotion leaves Sebastian more bemused than responsive: "I can no other answer make but thanks, / And thanks, and ever thanks" (3, 3, 15–16). Whether we are to take Antonio's affection as evidence of sexual attraction or exalted male friendship is not resolved. Whatever the truth, Antonio may be the one character who acts not from "self-love" but from affection for another.

Sebastian also discloses his personal history: "I do not without danger walk these streets" (3, 4, 27). He once fought successfully against Orsino and if discovered in this locale would be subject to retribution (3, 4, 37–39). Despite such risk, Antonio accepts Sebastian's purse, and the two agree to meet later. By now we are confident that mix-ups involving the twins are more likely than ever.

Almost at once these plot strands begin to meld. Before Malvolio enters, Olivia comments on Maria's report about his attire and behavior: "I am as mad as he, / If sad and merry madness equal be" (3, 4, 15–16). At last she acknowledges that extremes of emotion are also forms of madness, and as Malvolio flirts, struts, and grins according to instructions in the letter, she adds: "Why, this is midsummer madness!" (3, 4, 61). Yet even as he raves, she remains solicitous: "Let some of my people have a special care of him" (3, 4, 67). Her fundamental decency shines through.

Thinking his performance a triumph, Malvolio becomes haughtier with Sir Toby, Maria, and Fabian: "You are idle, shallow things. I am not of your element" (3, 4, 132–33). Fabian's response is telling: "If this were played upon a stage now, I could condemn it as an improbable fiction" (3, 4, 136–37). We feel the playwright's absolute confidence in his creation, as Fabian's remark turns into a form of "metatheater," in which the work of art comments on itself. Meanwhile, Malvolio's manner inspires an even more vicious prank, instigated, not surprisingly, by Sir Toby: "Come, we'll have him in a dark room and / bound" (3, 4, 144–45). The figurative madness we have witnessed will soon be treated as if it were literal.

Sir Andrew's entrance with a pretentious note of challenge meant for Cesario is ignored by Sir Toby, who intends to undermine his stooge by delivering the threat personally. That opportunity presents itself when Viola enters, pursued by Olivia, but Viola can barely escape when she is confronted by Sir Toby, eager to see a fight that he anticipates with mock pomposity:

> Therefore on,
> or strip your sword stark naked, for meddle you
> must, that's certain, or forswear to wear iron about
> you. (3, 4, 259–62)

The ironic implication is that, if Cesario won't fight, "he" is not a man. This entire encounter inspires comic terror, as both Viola and Sir Andrew quiver at the prospect of dueling an opponent reputed to be highly skilled. In Viola's words,

> A little thing
> would make me tell them how much I lack of a
> man. (3, 4, 314–16)

The entrance and exits here are superbly coordinated.

That fear turns into physical comedy, as the two incompetent fencers delicately wield their weapons, but the swordplay is abbreviated when interruptions come fast. First Antonio rescues Cesario (whom he mistakes for Sebastian); then the police arrest Antonio. The presence of the law, by the way, sends Sir Toby scurrying: "I'll be with you anon" (3, 4, 334). Why should he be so frightened? Perhaps Malvolio's estimation of him is right.

The more important drama, however, is between Antonio and Viola. The former demands that the money he earlier lent Sebastian be returned (3, 4, 356), but Viola naturally does not recognize him. Even so, she offers other money, but Antonio remains dumbfounded and as he is taken away shouts: "But O, how vile an idol proves this god! / Thou hast, Sebastian, done good feature shame" (3, 4, 384–85). Viola, however, senses the reason for his outrage: "Prove true, imagination, O, prove true, / That I, dear brother, be now ta'en for you!" (3, 4, 395–96). This play dramatizes all sorts of madness. Now Viola hopes that one manifestation comes true.

In 3, 4, Shakespeare dramatizes a remarkable range of emotions. We see the comic delusion of Malvolio; the petty bitterness of Sir Toby, Maria, and Fabian; the passion of Olivia; the alarm of Sir Andrew; the farce of the fight; and the loyalty and anger of Antonio, all swirling around the confusion, fear, and desire of Viola, who ricochets from one dizzying predicament to another.

Her bewilderment is soon shared by Sebastian, who arrives at Olivia's house, where he is mistaken by everyone for Viola. He banters with Feste, then tangles with Sir Toby, Sir Andrew, and Fabian, all of whom are shaken to find a more robust man than they left. Their fight has just started when Olivia enters and properly blames Sir Toby:

> Ungracious wretch,
> Fit for the mountains and the barbarous caves,
> Where manners ne'er were preached! Out of my
> sight! (4, 1, 48–51)

Olivia doesn't really grasp the reason for this squabble, but we don't mind because Sir Toby deserves whatever chastisement he gets.

She next turns to comfort Sebastian, whom she assumes to be the delicate Cesario. He is nonplussed but pleasantly so: "What relish is in this? How runs the stream? / Or I am mad, or else this is a dream" (4, 1, 63–64). The words *mad* and *dream* tell us that Sebastian is falling for sensations that have overtaken other characters. Thus he accepts her invitation: "Would thou'dst be ruled by me!" (4, 1, 67–68), and his answer suits this play perfectly: "Madam, I will" (4, 1, 69). Sebastian intuits that his fulfillment lies in submission to love, a lesson some characters here never learn.

The swift-moving action then shifts to Malvolio, imprisoned in a dark room and under control of Feste as Sir Topas, the curate. In response to Feste's bizarre questions, Malvolio struggles to establish his rationality: "I am no more mad than you are" (4, 2, 49–50). His shouts would have amused Shakespeare's audience, who enjoyed making sport of the insane, and if Malvolio remains outraged, then we, too, might laugh. But if his cries reflect genuine suffering, then the injustice of his plight will touch us. Oddly, although Malvolio cannot see him, Feste dresses for this occasion, as Maria notes (4, 2, 67–68). Apparently Feste plays to please only himself.

Sebastian's next soliloquy reaffirms the theme of madness: "And though 'tis wonder that enwraps me thus, / Yet 'tis not madness" (4, 3, 3–4). He has fallen in love quickly and perhaps unrealistically, but when Olivia espouses similar sentiments (4, 3, 23–32), we believe them, too. Such acceptance on our part, like our willingness to believe that male and female twins could be mistaken for each other, is endemic to the world of comedy. Furthermore, if we accept what we see here is benign madness (and that supposition is in the spirit of the play), their mutual infatuation and impulsive marriage fit within the bounds of theatrical reality.

Act 5 stretches our endurance, as Shakespeare delays the reunion of Viola and Sebastian almost to the breaking point. First Orsino, accompanied by Cesario, enters to see Olivia, but they are interrupted by police officers with Sebastian, whom Viola identifies as the man who rescued her and whom Orsino remembers from years back as a dangerous but brave fighter (5, 1,

47–55). Antonio then tells his own story, which includes what he considers a betrayal by Sebastian, whom he thought he had saved (5, 1, 78–83). Here narrative and drama blend seamlessly.

Finally Olivia enters, and for the first time she and Orsino are onstage together. Each reacts as we might expect. Olivia responds to Orsino's pledges by dismissing them with his own imagery of music and love:

> If it be aught to the old tune, my lord,
> It is as fat and fulsome to mine ear
> As howling after music. (5, 1, 109–11)

Orsino then unleashes his customary excess of feeling, this time threatening to hurt Olivia through Cesario: "I'll sacrifice the lamb that I do love / To spite a raven's heart within a dove" (5, 1, 133–34). From this point on, accusations, denials, and affirmations fly back and forth, until one line from Olivia brings everyone up short: "Cesario, husband, stay" (5, 1, 148).

When amid muddle and outrage the Priest arrives, Olivia's use of *darkness* (5, 1, 161) suggests that all the characters share some variation of Malvolio's current predicament: trapped by false accusations, trying to prove to one another (and perhaps to themselves) that they are not mad. This moment brings out the ugliest aspects of Orsino, who turns on Cesario: "O thou dissembling cub! What wilt thou be / When time hath sowed a grizzle on thy case?" (5, 1, 173–74).

Just when Viola's situation seems at its worst, Sir Andrew enters, wounded and accusing Cesario of causing the damage. Sir Toby, also battered, resists Sir Andrew's attempt at soothing him by turning on his erstwhile comrade: "Will you help?—an ass-head, and a coxcomb, and a knave, a thin-faced knave, a gull?" (5, 1, 216–17). At this release of Sir Toby's true feelings, Sir Andrew may well earn our compassion.

At last Sebastian appears, and all perplexities are sorted out. In Olivia's words at discovering two identical figures, "Most wonderful!" (5, 1, 236). Even if the actors playing Viola and Sebastian do not look very much alike, as will probably be the case, the discovery moves us, for not only are romantic entanglements resolved, but also a brother and sister who each thought the other dead are reunited. Even Orsino seems to understand his folly, as he says to Viola: "Boy, thou hast said to me a thousand times / Thou never shouldst love woman like to me" (5, 1, 279–80). Still, as the lovers pair off, we may feel less than satisfied, for courageous Viola certainly deserves better than unreliable Orsino.

Only one character is left to be freed: Malvolio, who is escorted in and demands apology:

> And, acting this in an obedient hope,
> Why have you suffered me to be imprisoned,
> Kept in a dark house, visited by the priest,

> And made the most notorious geck and gull
> That e'er invention played on? Tell me why. (5, 1, 362–66)

These lines, too, can be played for pathos, in which case the audience may wonder exactly what Malvolio did to warrant such cruel treatment. On the other hand, Malvolio may simply maintain in an overbearing attitude, so that we find his questions less poignant. After Feste amuses himself by attempting to read the letter in the spirit of a madman (5, 1, 305–6), Fabian unravels the plot, adding that Sir Toby and Maria are now married, a fitting union, for these two jokesters can now torment each other in perpetuity.

Malvolio's exit line is also intriguing: "I'll be revenged on the whole pack of you!" (5, 1, 401). Is it delivered with genuine malice or comic frustration? Either way, the line earns an expression of regret from Olivia: "He hath been most notoriously abused" (5, 1, 402). But if she delivers these words with a wink, as if inviting conspiratorial laughter from the others, Orsino's counsel to soothe Malvolio's feelings may seem insufficient, even callous.

Feste's final song is an antidote to the egotism that has dominated the previous action. His line "For the rain it raineth every day" (5, 1, 415) suggests that no matter what we do, noble or not, the world goes on, and because of the brevity of our lives, we are simultaneously laughable and sad. This split attitude toward human existence underlies *Twelfth Night*, as well as many of Shakespeare's comedies. They end with an affirmation of love, but sometimes the distress that precedes such a resolution leaves us unsettled. Therefore the feeling that often remains, as it does after *Twelfth Night*, is tempered happiness.

A Few Words About the Histories

Shakespeare's histories present a couple of pedagogic challenges. For one, students who take up the texts without sufficient historical background will be lost. A second is that, given this predicament, they may be more reluctant than usual to tackle stories and characters that seem remote and language that is definitely complex. As a result instructors might not want to risk assigning these works.

Experience suggests, however, that if the difficulties these plays pose are great, the rewards of studying them are greater. Therefore consider a prereading pep talk. Explain that even though the dialogue is suffused with unfamiliar names and arcane details, if students give the play in question a chance, they will almost certainly become absorbed in machinations that have innumerable parallels to our own day. And for those students who have even minimal curiosity about history, government, or law, the play will prove revelatory. The same may well apply to teachers.

Before examining any specific work, the next step should be to reflect on the history play genre, which almost always dramatizes familiar events. Audiences thus seek not only information about what actually occurred but also interpretation that deepens their understanding. Such was certainly the case for Shakespeare's onlookers, who already knew the outcome of the stories about to unfold onstage.

Don't hesitate to ask for modern examples of the form. Over the years responses have changed but recently have included *The Iron Lady*, featuring Meryl Streep's portrayal of British prime minister Margaret Thatcher, and Steven Spielberg's *Lincoln*. One theatrical work almost always mentioned is the musical *1776*, in which creators of the Declaration of Independence sing and dance their way to the climactic moment on July 4. Again, audiences know how events will resolve. The major point of interest is why and how they do.

Note as well that like virtually all playwrights who dramatize history, Shakespeare takes considerable liberty with facts. Characters who never met historically conduct lengthy discussions, while other figures who were historically dead show up years later. What concerned Shakespeare more than historical accuracy, and what should concern us, is how the works succeed theatrically, as well as the implications of his presentation.

Now to the immediate background of the plays. In that same prereading session and with a genealogical chart at the ready, explore the history of the main characters. Acknowledge Shakespeare's primary source (Holinshed's *Chronicles of England, Scotland, and Ireland*); then focus on Richard II's forebears and contemporaries. Don't overwhelm students with detail, but try to provide the essentials.

Explain that Shakespeare wrote two tetralogies dramatizing English history from 1398 to 1485. *Richard II* is the first play in the second tetralogy, often called the Henriad, and it includes *Henry IV, Parts 1* and *2*, and *Henry V*. That sequence, although completed second, tells the first part of the narrative. The tetralogy of *Henry VI, Parts 1, 2*, and *3*, plus *Richard III* concludes the story but was in fact written first, early in Shakespeare's career.

Next turn to Edward III, who ruled from 1312 to 1377 and conquered much of Scotland and France. Of his seven legitimate sons, the oldest, Edward the Black Prince (so named because of the color of his shield), would have succeeded to the throne, but died before his father, and laws of inheritance decreed that the next in the royal line was the oldest son of the oldest son. Thus to the distaste of virtually everyone at court, Richard II, aged ten, succeeded his grandfather, Edward III.

Before the play bearing his name begins in 1398, Richard's reign spanned more than twenty years. The period had bright moments, notably in 1381, when the King put down the so-called Peasants' Revolt by confronting the rebels. But his regime was also marked by his increased delight in luxury and for granting privileges to favorites. Therefore resentments that had started simmering as soon as the boy assumed the throne grew more heated, and in the years immediately preceding this play, Richard tightened his grip on power by ordering the murder of several nobles, including his uncle, the Duke of Gloucester. Here is where *Richard II* starts.

Finally, with the historical background clear, remind the group that they will be dealing with politicians, who are notorious for masking true feelings with polite verbiage. Consider, perhaps, how a member of Congress may address remarks to "my good friend, the gentleman from Kentucky," when in fact the speaker's real sentiments are far less charitable. Shakespeare's characters similarly use oratory to disguise animosity, and therefore even seemingly direct statements must be probed for insidious insinuations.

Once everyone is appropriately suspicious, the class is ready to read.

Chapter Five

Richard II

The full title of this play is *The Tragedy of King Richard the Second*, and one issue any class will confront is whether the work meets the standards of tragedy. The main character is alternately grandiose, charming, bullying, sad, and eloquent. Given such mutability of behavior and attitude, how does he regard himself? More important, how should we regard him?

As you begin analysis, the assumption here is that you've introduced the history play form and provided background to this story. Before the class starts to read, however, take time to explain the crisis presented in the initial scene, set in January 1398: accusations of treason between Henry Bolingbroke, the King's cousin, and Mowbray, Duke of Norfolk, who may be considered Richard's chief of staff and the one who knows literally where bodies are buried.

The opening passages are worth examining closely. Consider Richard's first words: "Old John of Gaunt, time-honored Lancaster, / Hast thou, according to thy oath and band" (1, 1, 1–2). What is the King implying? Speaking to his uncle, the oldest surviving son of Edward III and the richest, most respected man in the kingdom, the King confirms that Gaunt's powers are waning. Moreover, irrespective of personal feeling, Gaunt must obey the orders of his much younger nephew. Thus Richard luxuriates in his position, but we already suspect that he is ill-suited for it.

These impressions are reinforced when the King demands that Gaunt's son Bolingbroke and Mowbray be presented: "High stomached are they both and full of ire, / In rage deaf as the sea, hasty as fire" (1, 1, 19–20). He delights in metaphor, as well as in dramatizing the passion of the moment and his place at its center. Indeed, he appears more entertained by theatrics than wary of disclosure.

These two lines also include key images of the play, including fire, the highest of the four elements that were understood to comprise the natural world (the others were earth, water, and air) and which therefore represents the kingship itself. Throughout Shakespeare, that position is also symbolized by the lion, the noblest of the beasts; the eagle, the highest of the birds; and, most importantly, the sun, the highest of the heavenly bodies.

Before arguments are heard, Bolingbroke, known also as the Duke of Hereford, greets the King: "Many years of happy days befall / My gracious sovereign, my most loving liege" (1, 1, 21–22). The tone is respectful, but underneath we sense resentment. Then Mowbray tries to outdo his opponent:

> Each day still better other's happiness
> Until the heavens, envying earth's good hap,
> Add an immortal title to your crown. (1, 1, 23–25)

The sentiments are so exaggerated that Mowbray is obviously trying to curry favor, as Richard understands: "We thank you both. Yet one but flatters us" (1, 1, 26). Richard may be impolitic, but he knows something about the game. We, too, understand that as these men try to safeguard their welfare, they instinctively resort to duplicity.

Next, Bolingbroke accuses Mowbray: "Thou art a traitor and a miscreant, / Too good to be so and too bad to live" (1, 1, 40–41). In response Mowbray dares not shift blame to Richard but can only deny Mowbray's own complicity: "First, the fair reverence of your Highness curbs me / From giving reins and spurs to my free speech" (1, 1, 56–57). He adds that even though his accuser is a relative of the King (1, 1, 60), Mowbray cannot permit such lies to stand: "I do defy him, and I spit at him" (1, 1, 62). By throwing down his gage (glove), Bolingbroke sets aside his royal station and offers to fight Mowbray, but the latter merely picks up the gage to show a willingness to hear the truth (1, 1, 80–85).

Thereafter Bolingbroke's claims against Mowbray are aimed obliquely at the King, starting with "all the treasons for these eighteen years" (1, 1, 97). He then asserts various manners of financial corruption, as well as collusion in the death of the Duke of Gloucester, the King's uncle. Throughout the scene, the question of precisely who is responsible for which crimes stays murky; given the political pressures of his day, the playwright had to handle such subjects delicately.

Richard remains taken with the show before him: "How high a pitch his resolution soars!" (1, 1, 113). He also seeks to assure Mowbray of impartiality:

> Now by my scepter's awe I make a vow:
> Such neighbor nearness to our sacred blood
> Should nothing privilege him nor partialize
> The unstooping firmness of my upright soul. (1, 1, 122–25)

Entranced by symbols of power, the King does not grasp what this play dramatizes: the nature of kingship is on the cusp of change.

To return to this scene, despite the King's assurance, Mowbray knows that the scope of his testimony is limited. Nonetheless, he tries to defend himself, first recalling his service at Calais (1, 1, 130–36), then denying involvement in the death of Gloucester. He is careful, however, not to shift blame elsewhere until, seeing no alternative, he throws down his own gage to invite trial by combat (1, 1, 150–51), in which the winner was assumed to have told the truth.

Before Bolingbroke can respond, the King, perhaps fearing inadvertent exposure, suggests that the two find compromise: "Forget, forgive; conclude and be agreed" (1, 1, 160). When that resolution proves unacceptable to both, Richard tries to exert authority: "Rage must be withstood. / Give me his gage. Lions make leopards tame" (1, 1, 179–80). Mowbray, however, is not assured: "Mine honor is my life; both grow in one. / Take honor from me and my life is done" (1, 1, 188–89). He claims that he has devoted his life to Richard, but now the King will not let him fight to preserve his reputation.

Bolingbroke, too, believes that his integrity has been impugned: "O, God defend my soul from such deep sin! / Shall I seem crestfallen in my father's sight?" (1, 1, 193–94). With Mowbray and Bolingbroke at an impasse, the King asserts himself: "We were not born to sue, but to command" (1, 1, 202). He then orders that Mowbray and Bolingbroke undergo trial by combat, perhaps in the hope that both petitioners may be eliminated.

In 1, 2, opposition to the King is embodied by the Duchess of Gloucester, widow of the slain man, who demands that John of Gaunt, her brother-in-law, take action against the murderers: "To safeguard thine own life, / The best way is to venge my Gloucester's death" (1, 2, 37–38). Gaunt, however, refuses to oppose Richard: "Let heaven revenge, for I may never lift / An angry arm against His minister" (1, 3, 42–43). These lines affirm a crucial concept: that in medieval England, the kingship was understood to be divinely ordained, the linchpin between God and humanity. The throne is thus ostensibly inviolate.

The overriding question, then, is when and if Richard should be removed from office. At which juncture do his actions so threaten the welfare of the country that they warrant expulsion? And what price will the nation pay for such revolt? Moreover, this plea by the Duchess also reminds us that these events involve both political and personal drama; here she reinforces the link between the two.

In 1, 3, which historically took place months later, Richard revels in the rituals prior to combat. First Mowbray states his case (1, 3, 16–25), then Bolingbroke his own (1, 3, 35–41), until Richard grandly announces his intentions: "Cousin of Hereford, as thy cause is right, / So be thy fortune in this royal fight" (1, 3, 55–56). The King has already taken sides, and Mowbray knows that his petition is lost. We understand Richard's strategy because Mowbray knows too many secrets, but we censure such mistreatment of a loyal ally.

After Bolingbroke offers tribute, Mowbray attempts to defend himself:

> However God or fortune cast my lot,
> There lives or dies, true to King Richard's throne,
> A loyal, just, and upright gentleman. (1, 3, 85–87)

The rest of the speech is a plea for the King's support, but Richard harshly dismisses him (1, 3, 97–99). Just as the contest is about to begin, however, the King throws down his warder and abrogates the battle with an explanation that is staggering in its convolution (1, 3, 124–45), in which "peace" (1, 3, 133) "Might from our quiet confines fright fair peace" (1, 3, 139).

Such twisting of words suggests the King fears for his own security. He ends by pronouncing sentence, first on Bolingbrook: exile for ten years (1, 3, 141–45). Bolingbrook seems to accept the punishment but also returns a threat that we know will prove true: "Your will be done. This must my comfort be; / That sun that warms you here shall shine on me" (1, 3, 147). He guarantees that one day the crown will be his.

Instead of responding, Richard turns to Mowbray and exiles him for life (1, 3, 150–55). Understandably feeling betrayed by the monarch whom he has served so devotedly, Mowbray broods over his fate: "The language I have learnt these forty years, / My native English, now I must forgo" (1, 3, 161–62). His mourning is affirmation of the bond that unites national culture, language, and identity. After this request, the King's retort seems even crueler: "It boots thee not to be compassionate. / After our sentence plaining comes too late" (1, 3, 177–78).

Calling Mowbray and Bolingbroke together, the King demonstrates his political acuity by forbidding the two men from ever communicating with each other. Richard understands that in the face of a common enemy, two rivals could conspire against him. At such moments, inviting the class to find similar maneuvering among our own political leaders is almost irresistible.

In light of Mowbray's despair, Bolingbroke tries to catch him off guard: "Confess thy treasons ere thou fly the realm" (1, 3, 202). Bolingbroke hopes for an accidental slip that will implicate Richard, but Mowbray resists: "But what thou art, God, thou, and I do know, / And all too soon, I fear, the King shall rue" (1, 3, 208–9). He spares Richard the need to act.

Nonetheless, Richard does act, albeit unexpectedly: He reduces Bolingbroke's sentence to six years (1, 3, 215–16). Why is the King so generous? He claims that he senses Gaunt's "grievèd heart" (1, 3, 213), but whatever the reason, additional ministrations by Gaunt do not move the King further (1, 3, 239–41). Later Gaunt tries to soften Bolingbroke's pain of exile: "Look what thy soul holds dear, imagine it / To lie that way thou goest, not whence thou com'st" (1, 3, 292–93). His son, though, reacts realistically: "O no, the apprehension of the good / Gives but the greater feeling to the worse" (1, 3, 307–8). Such practicality becomes his chief political attribute.

In 1, 4, Richard sits among confederates, including Bagot, Green, and Aumerle, and ruminates on Bolingbroke's affinity for winning affection from the masses: "How he did seem to dive into their hearts / With humble and familiar courtesy" (1, 4, 26–27). The King is contemptuous of the commoners but also confirms that his position is becoming vulnerable to political forces.

This passage may inspire a detour from the play itself, as the class considers which politicians from our own era have such skills as Richard describes. You might particularly note that the ability to win popular support is independent of ideology or intellect. Remind the group, too, that many of the characters in Shakespeare's history plays have contemporary American analogues. Indeed, no matter which party or individual holds power, the conflicts dramatized in *Richard II* and other history plays endure.

Meanwhile Richard learns that John of Gaunt is on his deathbed, and here the King's malice becomes even more blatant: "Now put it, God, in the physician's mind / To help him to his grave immediately!" (1, 4, 60–61). Richard also disdains support from Gaunt's supporters: "The lining of his coffers shall make coats / To deck our soldiers for these Irish wars" (1, 4, 62–63). His vanity is crossing the line into illegality.

In 2, 1, the dying Gaunt pays tribute to his native land in terms that reinforce the religious imagery of the play: "This blessèd plot, this earth, this realm, this England" (2, 1, 55–56). He also emphasizes Richard's greed, describing England as "leased out" (2, 1, 65). Not long afterward, Richard struts in: "What comfort, man? How is 't with agèd Gaunt?" (2, 1, 78). The dying man tries to alert the King: "A thousand flatterers sit within thy crown" (2, 1, 106), then "Landlord of England art thou now, not king" (2, 1, 119). Gaunt thereby clarifies that the moral disease on the throne contaminates the country at large.

Nonetheless, Richard ignores these admonitions: "A lunatic, lean-witted fool, / Presuming on an ague's privilege" (2, 1, 122–23). At this juncture Gaunt is helpless, but before he is carried out, he compares Richard to a "too-long withered flower" (2, 1, 141), anticipating imagery that will prove prevalent. Moments later, Northumberland reports Gaunt's passing: "His tongue is now a stringless instrument" (2, 1, 157), echoing Mowbray's language (1, 3, 164), but Richard responds without feeling: "The ripest fruit first falls, and so doth he" (2, 1, 161).

Thereafter, the King descends to his nadir, confiscating the inheritance that, by all rights, belongs to Bolingbroke:

> Towards our assistance we do seize to us

> The plate, coin, revenues, and movables
> Whereof our uncle Gaunt did stand possessed. (2, 1, 168–70)

Such brazen illegality inspires the Duke of York, the last surviving son of Edward III, to reaffirm the fundamental law of primogeniture (inheritance by the oldest son): "Take Hereford's rights away, and take from time / His charters and his customary rights" (2, 1, 204–5). From this point on, York's loyalty is divided between the King, to whom he has sworn allegiance, and York's own nephew, Bolingbroke, who must endure disenfranchisement.

Images of time pervade this play, often in conjunction with images of music. Both represent order, the place of humanity in a universal system that during periods of turmoil is shattered. York implies that Richard has violated not only human rights but also divine right. Ultimately York supports the occupant of the throne, whoever that might be, but his protests here lead us to contemplate issues that dominate Shakespeare's history plays. What responsibilities does a ruler have toward the governed? What qualities do we want in a ruler? Does behavior of a ruler ever become so intolerable that usurpation of the throne is justified?

The king's capacity to ignore such danger is startling: "Think what you will, we seize into our hands / His plate, his good, his money, and his lands" (2, 1, 218–19). Then he reminds everyone that he intends to go to Ireland to quash a rebellion, but what Richard does not realize is that a more important rebellion is rising in his own country and that he is the target. Moreover, he compounds his error by leaving the nation under the control of York, who has just accused Richard of crimes against the family, the state, and God. Is Richard too proud to be realistic or just foolish?

Whatever the answer, he remains fascinating. He is innately theatrical and acts with a sense of his own loftiness. Yet we wonder why he proceeds as impudently as he does. Perhaps even at this point we recognize that circumstances have thrust him into a position for which he is unsuited, so that no matter how he poorly governs, we are still sympathetic. Thus the play's tragic potential.

We also tend to commiserate with someone who inspires so much resentment, as at the end of 2, 1, when three noblemen, Ross, Willoughby, and Northumberland, are left alone. All seek to move against the King, but none dares approach the subject directly, until Northumberland, a member of the influential Percy family, states: "The King is not himself, but basely led / By flatterers" (2, 1, 251–52). After Ross blames Richard for other difficulties, all three share concerns (2, 1, 269–82), until Ross speaks the inevitable:

> Be confident to speak, Northumberland.
> We three are but thyself, and speaking so
> Thy words are but as thoughts. Therefore be bold. (2, 1, 284–86)

Their unified front established, the trio sets out to overthrow the King.

In 2, 2, while Richard languishes in Ireland, his supporters, including the Queen and the elderly Duke of York, bemoan their situation. Although historically the Queen was but nine years old, here she becomes a voice of conscience:

> Yet again methinks
> Some unborn sorrow, ripe in Fortune's womb
> Is coming towards me. (2, 2, 9–11)

Her intimations are followed by Green's report that Bolingbroke and his forces have landed at Ravenspurgh (2, 2, 50–52).

The words of York are especially poignant:

> Here am I left to underprop his land,
> Who, weak with age, cannot support myself.
> Now comes the sick hour that his surfeit made;
> Now shall he try his friends that flattered him. (2, 2, 86–89)

The image of sickness and the theme of mistrust, both of which originate in Richard's words and actions, will continue, while York's divided loyalty, as articulated in 2, 2, 117–22, soon becomes shared by others. Indeed, impending disaster is apparent in the nervousness of Bushy, Bagot, and Green. In Green's words, "Besides, our nearness to the King in love / Is near the hate of those love not the King" (2, 2, 134–35). The only one blind to the threat is Richard.

In 2, 3, forces allied with Bolingbroke gather, including Northumberland and his son, Henry Percy, nicknamed Hotspur. The younger Percy here proclaims his allegiance to Bolingbroke (2, 3, 43–46), an ironic foreshadowing of *Henry IV, Part 1*, when Hotspur opposes the man he now supports. York, though, cannot control outrage at Bolingbroke's actions: "I am no traitor's uncle" (2, 3, 92). He continues: "Thou art a banished man and here art come, / Before the expiration of thy time" (2, 3, 114–15).

Bolingbroke explains the results of Richard's actions against him (2, 3, 123–26), then attempts to justify his unprecedented response:

> I am a subject,
> And I challenge law. Attorneys are denied me,
> And therefore personally I lay my claim
> To my inheritance of free descent. (2, 3, 137–40)

Because Richard has broken his unspoken covenant with the people, Bolingbroke believes that he is no longer bound by the King's decree. Yet York remains on the side of the King: "For I am loath to break our country's laws" (2, 3, 173).

Meanwhile, the question of how Shakespeare judges Bolingbroke's actions not only is at the core of the playwright's political beliefs but also anticipates events from our own day. Indeed, at this point, someone is likely to invoke Richard Nixon or Bill Clinton, leading the group to review how either man's transgressions led to impeachment. Such discussion again reinforces how these plays, though written and set in a distant age, remain timely.

In the next brief scene, we hear about chaos on Richard's side. In Salisbury's words: "Thy sun sets weeping in the lowly west" (2, 4, 21). Such disorder is contrasted with actions by Bolingbroke, who orders the execution of Bushy and Green (3, 1, 30–32), but his decisiveness raises questions about the kind of ruler we want. True, Bolingbroke evaluates Bushy and Green accurately, but he disposes of them ruthlessly. Is such determination an inevitable consequence of realpolitik?

In 3, 2, Richard defends his authority, but his vulnerabilities are apparent. First the Bishop of Carlisle, the voice of orthodox religion, affirms Richard's place: "Fear not, my lord. That power that made you king / Hath power to keep you king in spite of all" (3, 2, 27–28). Then Richard announces his own confidence in God:

> Not all the water in the rough rude sea
> Can wash the balm off from an anointed king.
> The breath of worldly men cannot depose
> The deputy elected by the Lord. (3, 2, 55–58)

For him, symbols of authority supersede the actuality. In addition, the images of fire and water signify Richard's kingship and its destruction by Bolingbroke.

Soon, however, reports of Bolingbroke's advances leave Richard ruminating helplessly: "Have I not reason to look pale and dead?" (3, 2, 80). Aumerle, York's son, tries to comfort Richard: "Remember who you are" (3, 2, 83), at which point Richard reasserts his authority: "I had forgot myself. Am I not king?" (3, 2, 84). He manages to view himself as both ruler and performer but then accuses his subjects: "They break their faith to God as well as us" (3, 2, 103). He thereby begins to embrace the role of royal victim.

With the news that Bushy, Bagot, and Green have made peace with Bolingbroke, the King calls them: "Three Judases" (3, 2, 136), not the only time he will compare himself to Jesus. But when he learns that his cohorts have been executed, his perspective changes: "For God's sake, let us sit upon the ground / And tell sad stories of the death of kings" (3, 2, 160–61). He also abandons his kingly pose:

> I live with bread like you, feel want,
> Taste grief, need friends. Subjected thus,
> How can you say to me I am a king? (3, 2, 180–82)

These lines contribute to a remarkable transformation of our view of Richard. Earlier we probably regarded him as a self-indulgent, corrupt ruler, willing to solidify power by any means. Now he understands that he has been thrust into circumstances where his personality clashes with his duties. In addition, Richard's references to his "hollow crown" (3, 2, 165) and a "little scene" (3, 2, 169) suggest that he recognizes how all along he has merely performed the role of King. He leaves with another insight: "He does me double wrong / That wounds me with the flatteries of his tongue" (3, 2, 223–24). At last he realizes how he has been deceived.

His performance continues in 3, 3, after Bolingbroke threatens to "lay the summer's dust with showers of blood" (3, 3, 44). Is such willingness to resort to slaughter a quality we should admire? Richard's appearance inspires wonder from York, who offers an apt metaphor: "Alack, alack for woe / That any harm should stain so fair a show!" (3, 3, 72–73). The King also draws comfort from his position:

> Yet know, my master, God omnipotent,
> Is mustering in his clouds on our behalf
> Armies of pestilence. (3, 3, 87–89)

Subsequent histrionics temporarily furnish Richard with a measure of triumph. First he ponders his motivation: "What must the King do now? Must he submit? / The King shall do it" (3, 3, 148–49). After mocking "King Bolingbroke" (3, 3, 178), Richard narrates his own performance: "Down, down I come, like glist'ring Phaëton" (3, 3, 183). Finally he calls out Northumberland: "Fair cousin, you debase your princely knee / To make the base earth proud with kissing it" (3, 3, 199–200). Thus the King is no political naïf. As long as he can revel in theatrics, he turns Bolingbroke into a crass conqueror and himself into a glorious martyr.

In 3, 4, Shakespeare inserts an apparently innocuous scene, this one featuring the gardener and his colleagues, who contemplate the state of the land they tend, both the local greenery and the nation as a whole: "He that hath suffered this disordered spring / Hath now himself met with the fall of leaf" (3, 4, 52–53). The image of the garden implies that a nation is a living organism whose political well-being reflects the stability of the crown. Yet even though we may feel sympathy for Richard, we must acknowledge that he has conducted himself badly.

Such complication increases in 4, 1, when Bolingbroke arranges a trial to justify his taking the throne. As Fitzwater, Aumerle, Bagot, and others squabble over evidence of the King's misdeeds, including his treatment of Mowbray, Bolingbroke demonstrates his political adroitness by allowing those who might band together against him to bog themselves down in argument. Soon the Bishop of Carlisle enters and berates Bolingbroke's supporters:

> My Lord of Hereford here, whom you call king,
> Is a foul traitor to proud Hereford's king,
> And if you crown him, let me prophesy
> The blood of English shall manure the ground

> And future ages groan for this foul act. (4, 1, 140–44)

He adds:

> O, if you raise this house against this house,
> It will the woefullest division prove
> That ever fell upon this cursèd earth! (4, 1, 151–53)

Carlisle is predicting events that Shakespeare's audience knew were coming, so here is the moment to clarify them for the class. After Bolingbroke assumed the throne as Henry IV, he ruled for eleven strife-filled years, then was succeeded by his son, Henry V. After his short reign, which included the famous Battle of Agincourt, in which the undermanned English defeated the vastly more powerful forces of France, Henry V died, leaving his nine-month-old son on the throne.

During Henry VI's childhood, rival "protectors" from the Beaufort family (descended from illegitimate sons of Gaunt) sought to control him and the government, but even after Henry VI matured, he proved hapless, and factions representing the families of Lancaster (offspring of Gaunt and symbolized by the red rose) and York (symbolized by the white rose) plotted and battled in the dynastic struggle known as the Wars of the Roses.

That internecine conflict began in 1455 and lasted approximately thirty years, through the reigns of York descendants Edward IV and the infamous Richard III. The latter succeeded to the throne by murdering his older brothers, then during his bloody two-year rule did away with his nephews (the notorious "Princes in the Tower"). Again, a glance at the genealogy chart used earlier will clarify the story, which Shakespeare dramatized in the first tetralogy that includes *Henry VI, Parts 1, 2,* and *3* and *Richard III.* (Additional questions about succession are raised in *Henry IV, Part 1* and further explored in chapter 6 on that play).

The turmoil ended in 1485 with the ascension of Henry VII, whose marriage to Elizabeth Woodville united the York and Lancaster factions. Summarizing these events should lead to consideration of the longstanding view that Shakespeare understood the Wars of the Roses to be punishment visited on England because of Bolingbroke's usurpation of the throne and the necessary expiation of sin.

In response to this interpretation, and given Richard II's crimes and the decades of turmoil that followed, consider how Shakespeare dramatizes the deposing of Richard from multiple viewpoints. True, Richard abuses his power and fails to fulfill his responsibilities, but as Carlisle warns, Bolingbroke's overthrow is also a violation. Yet Bolingbroke's actions change the nature of the kingship and begin to bring England out of the medieval age into the modern era. On the other hand, Bolingbroke acts wrongly, but then Richard does as well. And so on. How to balance these conflicting perspectives?

Throughout the rest of act 4, Richard relinquishes the throne with ever greater flair. He recalls those who supported him: "Did they not sometime cry 'All Hail' to me? / So Judas did to Christ" (4, 1, 177–78). He dangles the crown as if it were a prize and Bolingbroke a child reaching for it (4, 1, 190–91). When Richard actually removes his crown, he intimates that only a lawful king can do so: "All pomp and majesty I do forswear" (4, 1, 220). He even pronounces a blessing on Bolingbroke: "God save King Henry, un-kinged Richard says" (4, 1, 229). And when ordered to read a list of charges, he feigns inability to see: "Mine eyes are full of tears" (4, 1, 255).

One passage that demands examination is 4, 1, 288–300, when the King stares into the looking glass while echoing lines from Marlowe's *Dr. Faustus*, then smashes the glass to the ground. The gesture embodies both fascination with performance as well as frustration that it is just that: a performance. Bolingbroke's last attempt to salvage dignity is his branding Richard with the word *shadow* (4, 1, 303–4), but the King undermines this effort with another flight of verbal fancy (4, 1, 305–11). Even though Richard is defeated, he acknowledges his loss with a flourish that dwarfs everyone else.

In 5, 1, when the King and Queen meet before they are separated, Richard retains his sense of the dramatic: "Tell thou the lamentable tale of me, / And send the hearers weeping to their beds" (5, 1, 45–46). Several lines later, after Northumberland enters to lead Richard to Pomfret Castle, from where almost no one returns (5, 1, 53–54), the former King responds to what is essentially a death sentence by warning Northumberland about the newly enthroned Henry IV: "He shall think that thou, which knowest the way / To plant unrightful kings, wilt know again" (5, 1, 63–64). The accuracy of this prediction is further evidence of Richard's acumen.

In 5, 2, the familial conflict predicted by Carlisle becomes manifested in the quarrel between York and his son, Aumerle. While the father, always loyal to the throne, now stands with King Henry, Aumerle remains allied with Richard and therefore is forced by his father to surrender a letter that reveals Aumerle's participation in a conspiracy against the new King. Here the crisis in political life extends into the family, as York must again decide where to place his allegiance. Despite his wife's protests (5, 2, 97–103), York follows the fundamental principle of his existence and leads his son to Henry.

Before that meeting, the King inquires about his own "unthrifty son" (5, 3,1), said to frequent taverns of London amid "unrestrainèd loose companions" (5, 3, 7). That query probably brought smiles to the faces of Shakespeare's audience, who knew about the man nicknamed Hal, eventually England's most celebrated monarch, Henry V. (If they anticipated one companion in particular, Falstaff, their grins would doubtless have broadened.) They also understood that Henry's fears about his son's remaining a feckless reprobate will prove unfounded. We in turn can only wonder which portion of this tetralogy was already percolating in Shakespeare's mind.

In the next scene, York brings before Henry charges of treachery against Aumerle, but the new King acts mercifully: "I pardon him, as God shall pardon me" (5, 3, 137). The sequence confirms that chaos has been unleashed by the usurpation. Throughout the two subsequent plays that bear his name, King Henry struggles to maintain control, but his reign is scarred by political argument, bloody battles, and his own physical debilitation. Again, the relationship between the health of the kingship and that of the country at large is paramount.

In the next brief scene, Exton takes the new King's words and glances to mean one thing: Henry wants Richard dead. Is that inference correct? We cannot say, but in any case Exton decides that he is the man to carry out the murder: "I am the King's friend and will rid his foe" (5, 4, 12). Thus he represents forces of vengeance that do not disappear with the ascension of Henry but that remain part of the task of securing power.

In Richard's final soliloquy, he is still the performer but also the audience, more concerned with poetry than reality: "I have been studying how I may compare / This prison where I live unto the world" (5, 5, 1–2). Moreover, he speaks with a new self-understanding:

> Sometimes I am king.
> Then treasons make me wish myself a beggar,
> And so I am; then crushing penury
> Persuades me I was better when a king. (5, 5, 32–35)

Throughout this play he has grappled with his identity, but at this moment he finally acknowledges that he has never known not only who he was but also who he wanted to be. One other telling line is: "I wasted time, and now doth time waste me" (5, 5, 50), an elegant echo of a sentiment offered earlier by the gardener, who spoke of the "waste of idle hours" (3, 4, 72).

Richard again evokes images of music and time, both of which reflect the natural order that has been broken by his own behavior and Henry's seizing the throne. This passage also leads to the question of whether, despite the full title of the play, Richard II ever achieves the tragic stature of, for example, Hamlet or Lear. Some critics claim that he does not because other tragic heroes in Shakespeare and elsewhere fight against forces that oppose them, while Richard is ultimately passive. Students, however, rarely leave this perspective unchallenged.

Visited by the groom, Richard speaks with new modesty, addressing him as "noble peer" (5, 5, 69). Richard even forgives his horse, Barbary, for allowing Henry to ride him because Richard accepts that he, too, was subdued: "I was not made a horse, / And yet I bear a burden like an ass" (5, 5, 94–95). As for the killing of Richard, it is historically inaccurate in that he probably was left to starve to death. Here, however, he dies romantically in a spasm of violence, so that even Exton is impressed: "As full of valor as of royal blood" (5, 5, 117).

Richard II concludes with Henry's dispensation of justice. He pardons Fitzwater and Carlisle, whom he judges to have acted in the best interests of the kingdom, but condemns others whom he believes have behaved selfishly and still threaten the crown. He also expresses regret over Exton's murder of Richard and as penance promises a journey to the Holy Land, but that excursion is one he never undertakes.

This passage leads directly to the opening of *Henry IV, Part 1*, which ideally should follow the reading of this play. It builds on the foundation established in *Richard II* and is highlighted by the humor and humanity of the irresistible Falstaff. Whatever the class schedule, any presentation of *Richard II* should end with affirmation of two dominant themes. One concerns the qualities necessary for effective rule. The other is the personal clash between Richard, Shakespeare's last feudal king, and Henry, who led the English monarchy into the modern age and whose strategies as yet permeate the politics of our day.

Chapter Six

Henry IV, Part 1

Henry IV, Part 1 works most effectively when studied immediately after *Richard II*, so that students can approach this work with the background necessary to understand the characters and their motivations. But if *Henry IV* is being read independently, you will need to provide the information (and perhaps inspiration) offered here in "A Few Words about the Histories," then recapitulate events that take place in *Richard II*, and finally set up the opening of this play.

It begins in 1402, two years after the death of Richard II, and from the initial lines we realize how the political environment has changed:

> No more the thirsty entrance of this soil
> Shall daub her lips with her own children's blood.
> No more shall trenching war channel her fields. (1, 1, 5–7)

The King understands that the internal warfare currently besetting England is the consequence of his usurpation of the throne (1, 1, 11–16). *Richard II* ends with Henry's vow to visit the Holy Land as penance for this crime, necessary though it might have been, but the journey is one he never takes.

The crisis the king faces is caused by former advocates who helped him gain the throne and now seek greater influence. One of them, Mortimer, had been fighting the notorious Welshman Glendower but has been captured (1, 1, 38–41). The King, however, refuses to ransom him for reasons that will be apparent later. Here the more important point is that Henry understands how he owes these men but still must resolve the awkward task of satisfying their ambition without eroding his authority. The same qualities that drove him to take power now drive him to consolidate it, a challenge faced by any new officeholder.

One offstage character is mentioned: Henry Percy (nicknamed Hotspur), Mortimer's brother-in-law and the son of Northumberland, both strong supporters of the former Henry Bolingbroke against Richard II. One reason the King resents Hotspur is the latter's refusal to release prisoners (1, 1, 70–75, 93–94), but Westmoreland assigns this decision to Hotspur's uncle Worcester (1, 1, 95). Henry's willingness to wait for more evidence reinforces a fundamental tension of his reign: political debt versus effective rule.

A more painful cause of the King's discomfort is the contrast between Hotspur and the King's own son, also named Henry and called Hal. The King regards Hotspur as:

> sweet Fortune's minion and her pride;
> Whilst I, by looking on the praise of him,
> See riot and dishonor stain the brow
> Of my young Harry. (1, 1, 82–85)

This speech sets up one great irony of this play, for the Elizabethan audience would have known the legend about the wastrel Hal, who, in the manner of the Prodigal Son, returns to the fold and eventually becomes the celebrated Henry V. We also hear about the relationship between Hotspur and honor, a recurring theme here.

Mention of Hal takes us to the other prime setting of the play: the lower-class dens of London. The court and the tavern become the two ways of life that Hal must synthesize within himself. The scene also introduces us to what may be Shakespeare's most remarkable creation, Sir John Falstaff, whose first words establish his singular attitude: "Now, Hal, what time of day is it, lad?" (1, 2, 1). Although he is addressing the Prince of Wales, the future King of England, Falstaff's irreverence recognizes no sovereignty. Meanwhile Hal's boisterous jesting shows how profoundly he prizes this man.

The character has two vague historical precedents. One is Sir John Oldcastle, an associate of Hal's and a successful soldier. The other is Sir John Fastolfe, who appears briefly in *Henry VI, Part 1*, in which the playwright unfairly brands him a coward. Political considerations from noble families prevented use of either real name. Nonetheless, we should think of Falstaff as largely a product of Shakespeare's imagination: grotesquely fat and a composite of, among other qualities, wit, lust, and self-indulgence. Even after Hal becomes king and circumstances compel him to abandon Falstaff the man, Hal will embrace lessons learned from Falstaff, the spiritual force.

As an admitted thief and drunkard, Sir John makes no apology for his life:

> and let men say we be men of good government,
> being governed, as the sea is, by our noble
> and chaste mistress the moon, under whose countenance
> we steal. (1, 2, 28–31)

His reference to good government underlies the disparate worlds of this play. Just as King Henry and his forces stole the crown under the authority of the "sun" (one symbol of the kingship), so Falstaff and his cronies steal by the moon. Falstaff's men are simply honest about their profession.

Despite the banter with Hal, Falstaff carries no illusions about the role his chum will one day perform: "Do not, when thou art king, hang a thief" (1, 2, 65–66). To which Hal replies, "No, thou shalt" (1, 2, 67). No matter how warm their friendship, both men understand that eventually Hal must leave Falstaff behind. At this moment, however, Hal conspires with Poins to steal from Falstaff after another robbery at Gadshill:

> The virtue of this jest will be the
> incomprehensible lies that this same fat rogue will
> tell us when we meet at supper. (1, 2, 192–94)

When Hal is left alone, though, another aspect of his personality emerges in one of the key speeches not only of this play, but of the entire Henriad: "I know you all, and will awhile uphold / The unyoked humor of your idleness" (1, 2, 202–3). He calculates every word and move. In the next line, he compares himself to the sun, then articulates his political strategy:

> My reformation, glitt'ring o'er my fault,
> Shall show more goodly and attract more eyes
> Than that which hath no foil to set it off. (1, 2, 220–22)

Is he merely deceptive, or is he also clever? Both, probably. In any case, from this point on, even when he interacts with Falstaff, can we ever trust him? Do we ever like him? For that matter, how much do we need to like the individual who leads us if that person does the job well?

The scene moves back to the royal setting, where Henry tries to tamp down restlessness among his nobles. As Worcester says:

> Our house, my sovereign liege, little deserves
> The scourge of greatness to be used on it,
> And that same greatness too which our own hands
> Have holp to make so portly. (1, 3, 10–13)

The irony is that by deposing Richard, Henry unleashed forces that initially helped him but now threaten him. Worcester does not regard Henry as divinely ordained but merely as another politician. In response, the King expels Worcester from the room, a gesture meant to reaffirm strength yet which only reflects insecurity.

It also brings forth a new voice: that of Hotspur. Every other speaker treads carefully, but he spews forth words furiously in a manner that befits his nickname. For instance, his narrative about a seemingly effeminate soldier intruding on him during battle (1, 3, 30–71) reflects both Hotspur's courage and his intolerance for anyone who does not conform to his ideals.

Thus when the King disparages Mortimer, Hotspur fights back:

> Revolted Mortimer!

> He did never fall off, my sovereign liege,
> But by the chance of war. (1, 3, 95–97)

Hotspur, too, regards the King as no more than first among equals. Historically, Hotspur was only a couple of years younger than Henry IV, but Shakespeare makes Hotspur and Hal of the same generation to contrast Hotspur's braggadocio with Hal's apparent dissolution and political craft.

When Henry leaves, the Percies (Hotspur, Worcester, and Northumberland) ponder why the King would not ransom Mortimer. Recalling Richard as "that sweet lovely rose" (1, 3, 179), Hotspur suggests,

> But soft, I pray you. Did King Richard then
> Proclaim my brother Edmund Mortimer
> Heir to the crown? (1, 3, 158–60)

Now we understand that the King's reluctance to conduct this rescue is founded on the matter of succession, an issue tangled here because Shakespeare follows his source, Holinshed, and conflates two men named Mortimer into one.

Sir Edmund Mortimer, brother of Hotspur's wife, was captured by Glendower and later married the Welshman's daughter. The other Sir Edmund Mortimer was named by childless Richard II as heir apparent to the throne. If the class cares for additional detail, mention that because heir apparent Mortimer was descended from Lionel, Duke of Clarence, third son of Edward III, while Henry IV was a son of John of Gaunt, the fourth son, Mortimer may have had a stronger claim to the throne.

More complications existed. Heir apparent Mortimer's daughter Anne married Richard, Earl of Cambridge, a son of the Duke of York, seventh son of Edward III. After the death of Mortimer in 1424, the question loomed as to who was entitled to rule England: descendants of John of Gaunt (family name Lancaster) or descendants of Cambridge (family name York). Though the matter would seem comparatively straightforward (descendants of the older son have priority), Cambridge's claim was bolstered because he married Anne, like her father, of course, descended from Clarence, the third son. Moreover, the entire matter was muddled further over whether succession to the throne could pass through a woman.

Such intricate rules continually cast doubt on the legitimacy of Henry IV, as well as that of his son Henry V and especially that of his grandson, Henry VI, and decades later the arguments led to the Wars of the Roses (see chapter 5 on *Richard II*). How deeply you want to probe these issues depends on the interest shown by the class and the time available for digression.

To return to the play at hand, as resentment against Henry builds, Hotspur's speeches become more impassioned, almost to the point of raving: "By heaven, methinks it were an easy leap / To pluck bright honor from the pale-faced moon" (1, 3, 206–7). He speaks of honor not as personal morality, but as public acclaim. Thus we understand Hotspur to be symbolic of a chivalric spirit as outdated as the feudal world it complements.

Eventually Worcester calms his nephew, who still refers to the King as "this vile politician, Bolingbroke" (1, 3, 250), and the three plan to move against the King by releasing Hotspur's Scottish prisoners, who will join the fight again Henry. So will troops of Archbishop Scroop, whose brother was executed by the King. As this conspiracy forms, we think of Hal and Poins and their comparatively trivial plot against Falstaff. Hotspur's parting words are meant to inspire: "O let the hours be short / Till fields and blows and groans applaud our sport" (1, 3, 312–13). Yet he sounds manic, and no matter how justified these men believe themselves to be, this attempt to overthrow Henry appears small-minded and vengeful.

The plot against Falstaff is carried out in 2, 2. As he rumbles along, having lost his horse, he prepares to carry out the robbery: "A plague upon it when thieves cannot be true to one another!" (2, 2, 27–28), drawing another parallel with events at court. After the thievery is completed, as Falstaff shouts encouragement, he himself is robbed by the prince and Poins, and one of his reactions is particularly telling: "young men must live" (2, 2, 94–95). Falstaff is a drunk, a thief, a parasite, a cheat, and a lecher, but he still thinks of himself as young, and in some ways he indeed embodies the license of youth. At the same time, youth must be outgrown, and that realization is ever present.

Such understanding is contrasted with the impetuosity of Hotspur, who in the next scene broods over a letter from a lord reluctant to conspire against the King. Soon Hotspur's wife complains that even in his sleep he seems preoccupied with battle, but he refuses to reveal details (2, 3, 116–18). A penchant for secrecy usually betokens a guilty conscience, so no matter how brave his front, Hotspur may realize the fundamental misjudgment on which he is about to embark.

Act 2, scene 4 is one of the great scenes in all of Shakespeare. It begins with an exchange between Hal and Poins, in which the Prince reveals that he is aware of the power and reputation of his notorious rival: "I am not yet of Percy's mind, the Hotspur of the north" (2, 4, 104–5). Hal mocks Hotspur's capacity for violence, but more and more we anticipate their personal competition that we suspect will end in combat.

Falstaff then barrels in, exhausted yet overflowing with passion:

> There lives not
> three good men unhanged in England, and one of
> them is fat and grows old. (2, 4, 133–35)

After denizens of the tavern gather around him, he recounts in hilarious exaggeration how he was robbed: "A hundred upon poor four of us" (2, 4,

167–68). As he describes his valor, however, and under Hal's relentless questioning, details keep changing amid brilliantly phrased insults.

Hal finally demands the truth: "These lies are like their father that begets them" (2, 4, 234–35). The use of *father* suggests the deeper relationship between Hal and Falstaff. Soon Hal and Poins explain that they perpetrated the thievery and that Falstaff in fact ran away. Still, the fat knight remains unflappable: "By the Lord, I knew you as well as he that made you" (2, 4, 278–79), then adds: "The lion will not touch the true prince" (2, 4, 282–83). By using *lion*, traditionally a symbol of the King, Falstaff implies that not only he is a second father to Hal but also a king in his own right: lord of the tavern.

When news arrives of impending military action, Falstaff asks if Hal is afraid of Hotspur, but Hal claims that he has none of Falstaff's "instinct" (2, 4, 282–84). The query, however, sparks some hint of conscience in Hal, who orders: "Do thou stand for my father and examine me upon the particulars of my life" (2, 4, 387–88). To the delight of his listeners, Falstaff assumes mock trappings of office and begins the impersonation. Here is a moment to quote Oscar Wilde's line from *The Critic as Artist* (1891): "Man is least himself when he talks in his own person. Give him a mask, and he will tell you the truth."

Falstaff plays his role with zest, interrogating Hal in the voice of the King:

> If then thou be
> son to me, here lies the point: why, being son to
> me, art thou so pointed at? (2, 4, 419–21)

Multiple levels of meaning are at work. Falstaff knows that this question torments the King but also that Hal is aware of his father's anger. Amid raucous laughter from the company, Falstaff turns to his own defense and describes a "goodly portly man" (2, 4, 435) in Hal's circle:

> If then the tree may be
> known by the fruit, as the fruit by the tree, then
> peremptorily I speak it: there is virtue in that
> Falstaff; him keep with, the rest banish. (2, 4, 441–44)

Falstaff regards Hal as his offspring, and Hal's success would be Falstaff's own. Thus Falstaff is playing but also pleading not to be forgotten.

Hal is thereby inspired to switch roles: "Do thou stand for me, and I'll play my father" (2, 4, 447–48). From this point on, the potential king in Hal emerges, and as he assaults himself as played by Falstaff, his language becomes sharper:

> There is a devil haunts
> thee in the likeness of an old fat man. A tun of man
> is thy companion. (2, 4, 463–65)

While the insults become more disparaging and serious implications lurk, we can imagine the onlookers as well as Falstaff himself growing uncomfortable.

Finally the Prince concludes: "That villainous abominable misleader of youth, Falstaff, that old white-bearded Satan" (2, 4, 479–80). Falstaff as Hal offers a defense, both funny and moving. It begins with recognition of Falstaff's mortality: "That he is old, the more the pity; his white hairs do witness it" (2, 4, 485–86), then ends with a supplication: "Banish plump Jack, and banish all the world" (2, 4, 497–98). The line is a warning that Hal must never lose the humanity Falstaff has taught him, but Hal's icy reply confirms that he knows precisely what else must happen: "I do, I will" (2, 4, 499).

If time permits showing any scene from this play, 2, 4, is the one to choose. Analysis alone can never do it justice.

The rest of the episode reveals that Hal retains his capacity for mischief, as he misleads the sheriff who chases Falstaff. Hal is no paragon, but neither is he immoral or cruel. Later in combat, he will be heroic. Yet after his soliloquy in 1, 2, he never again opens up to us, and we must guess what he thinks. This consideration might lead to additional discussion. Can any successful politician afford to reveal what lies behind the image? Do we ever know what our leaders privately feel? Shakespeare's implication is that ruthless self-control is a political necessity.

Opposite qualities are apparent in the next scene, as the rebels gather to decide strategy, but from the start their egos are on display. When Glendower, now part of the team, boasts: "I can call spirits from the vasty deep" (3, 1, 55), Hotspur dismisses him: "Why, so can I, or so can any man, / But will they come when you do call for them?" (3, 1, 56–57). When tempers settle, the rebels dicker over how the country will be apportioned once they have triumphed (3, 1, 77–84). The discussion then degenerates into petty quarreling (3, 1, 120–24), confirming that the rebels' ultimate goal is not to provide for the good of the country but to satisfy their own greed.

When Glendower leaves briefly, Worcester admonishes Hotspur for his temper: "In faith, my lord, you are too willful-blame" (3, 1, 182), and warns about the dangers of his immoderate attitude. The lesson is one Hotspur never learns and further contrasts him with Hal. We enjoy Hotspur's impassioned behavior, but we understand that his instability makes him unreliable. We may dislike Hal's manipulation, even of those he befriends, but we respect the self-discipline that will make him a superior leader.

After a romantic interlude between Mortimer and his wife, including singing that briefly inspires a softer side of Hotspur, the play moves to the long-awaited encounter between King Henry and Hal. The essence of the scene is Henry's attempt to justify his past and make Hal act to ease Henry's burden, but first the King reveals the depths of his conscience:

> I know not whether God will have it so
> For some displeasing service I have done,
> That, in His secret doom, out of my blood
> He'll breed revengement and a scourge for me. (3, 2, 5–8)

Of course, the king knows precisely what he has done: overthrown Richard.

Henry also clarifies that Hal's behavior is turning him into that divine punishment the King endures:

> The hope and expectation of thy time
> Is ruined, and the soul of every man
> Prophetically do forethink thy fall. (3, 2, 38–40)

What follows is an extended justification for the usurpation: "And then I stole all courtesy from heaven" (3, 2, 52). We cannot be certain whether the king fears more for his country or for himself. Either way, he seeks pardon from his son, the only person to whom he can confess without fear of retribution. Such is the isolation of power. The King also seems to pursue assurance that he has succeeded as father and monarch, but that expression does not come here.

Instead Hal answers directly: "I shall hereafter, my thrice gracious lord, / Be more myself" (3, 2, 94–95). The line echoes an earlier sentence by Henry, when he cautioned the Percies: "I will from henceforth rather be myself" (1, 3, 5). But even as Henry tries to rouse Hal more by dramatizing the threat posed by Hotspur, Hal responds with the self-possession we have come to expect from him: "I will redeem all this on Percy's head" (3, 2, 137). His repetition of *honor* (3, 2, 144, 147) suggests that he is mocking Hotspur, but we also hear no expression of love for the King. Hal simply intends to fulfill the military and political duties demanded of him.

Even so, Henry remains burdened: "A hundred thousand rebels die in this" (3, 2, 165). He reminds us that the greatest responsibility any leader bears is the decision to send soldiers into battle. Henry also seems apprehensive that forces opposed to him will bring him down. Indeed, by the end of *Henry IV, Part 2*, the King will die from a physical disease like leprosy, as well as from spiritual exhaustion. At this moment, however, as if on cue, Sir Walter Blunt enters to report that the opposition is gathering strength. Pressure on Henry is unrelenting.

The next scene takes us to the tavern, where momentous events in court are contrasted with the buffoonery inherent in a way of life Hal must abandon. Without Hal's company, Falstaff is reduced to aimless philosophizing, but some of it shows insight, as when he refers to himself as "out of all order, out of all compass" (3, 3, 21). The phrases refer not only to his girth but also to the excess of his life.

The petty quarrel over who picked Falstaff's pocket (another parallel to thievery in the highest echelons of government) is interrupted by the entrance of Hal, who admits to having paid Falstaff's debt, but their laughter fades in the face of more important business. War is now imminent, and Falstaff, whom we may forget is a knight, must participate. In Hal's words: "I have procured thee, Jack, a charge of foot" (3, 3, 197). Reality is intruding on these men, and with Hal about to assume his rightful role, their separation draws closer.

As preparations for war continue, Hotspur, described by Douglas with unintentional irony as the "king of honor" (4, 1, 10), learns that his father, Northumberland, is ill. We remember Henry's expression of illness in the opening lines of the play, and now disease seems to be spreading. Hotspur, however, refuses to be discouraged:

> Yet doth he give us bold advertisement
> That with our small conjunction we should on
> To see how fortune is disposed to us. (4, 1, 39–41)

Why is he eager to fight? The answer comes a few lines later. Yet the entire discussion confirms that war is not simply a military exercise but also inflicts widespread consequences.

Worcester remains leery of going to battle without Northumberland:

> This absence of your father's draws a curtain
> That shows the ignorant a kind of fear
> Before not dreamt of. (4, 1, 76–78)

Hotspur naturally disagrees, and here we learn why: "It lends a luster, and more great opinion, / A larger dare, to our great enterprise" (4, 1, 81–82). His enthusiasm confirms that Hotspur fights primarily for personal acclaim, while Worcester, even though a relentless plotter, puts the cause first. But their disagreement raises a larger point: inherent in any rebellion is dissent. If these men can overthrow a king, as they did Richard, they will not hesitate to turn on one another.

Vernon then enters with news about Hal, who has dressed for war (4, 1, 110–16). The description carries such power that Hotspur cuts Vernon off. Yet Hotspur is so inflamed to fight that he immediately rallies his forces: "Come, let us take a muster speedily. / Doomsday is near. Die all, die merrily" (4, 1, 141–42). Hotspur is a dashing figure, but his lust for combat is mindless. As he prepares his campaign for individual glory, he gives no thought to the thousands who will die.

Shakespeare, however, does, and in the next scene we meet a ragtag bunch of soldiers who were unable to bribe Falstaff and thereby escape being pressed into service. Falstaff acknowledges that his recruits are a miserable bunch, and Hal agrees: "I never did see such pitiful rascals" (4, 2, 65). But Falstaff dismisses them:

> Tut, tut, good enough to toss; food for powder,

food for powder. They'll fill a pit as well as
better. Tush, man, mortal men, mortal men. (4, 2, 66–68)

Here is the darkest side of war: Poor, uninfluential men fight and die to satisfy the whims of rich, powerful men. Here, too, Falstaff loses some of his charm, for his corruption will cost most of these men their lives.

When we return to the formal aspects of conflict, leaders from the two sides meet to clarify the reasons for conflict. Sir Walter Blunt can barely tolerate the encounter: "You stand against anointed majesty" (4, 3, 46). How ironic that the same argument was used in support of Richard II. Hotspur then delineates a long list of grievances (4, 3, 58–94), but the essence is clear: the rebels who helped Bolingbroke become Henry IV have not received the spoils that they believe they deserve.

After Blunt casts aside this accusation, Hotspur harkens back to the memory of Richard II, another irony: "In short time after, he deposed the King, / Soon after that deprived him of his life" (4, 3, 97–98). The list of supposed malfeasances grows, but all are crimes against the rebels themselves, not violations of law. Thus this war is inspired not by patriots but by disappointed power brokers.

In the final scene of act 4, the Archbishop of York reflects on the already disheartened rebel army: "I fear the power of Percy is too weak / To wage an instant trial with the King" (4, 4, 19–20). The Archbishop also emphasizes the sickness that has infiltrated their forces, so that even Mortimer has retreated. Sir Michael tries to bolster the Archbishop's spirits by pointing to other eminent figures leading the rebellion, but when we learn that King Henry has gathered additional stalwart combatants, Hotspur's boasting looms more foolish and the fate of Falstaff's bedraggled company more dismal.

We move next to the battle of Shrewsbury, fought in July 1403. From his opening lines, the King sounds reluctant to fight: "How bloodily the sun begins to peer / Above yon bulky hill" (5, 1, 1–2). When, however, Worcester puts forth a familiar litany of Henry's actions against his former allies (5, 1, 31–72), the King grows angry: "And never yet did insurrection want / Such water colors to impaint his cause" (5, 1, 80–81). Despite his awareness of the inevitable price of battle, the King's pride supersedes his common sense.

Hal warns against the extent of the bloodshed to follow (5, 1, 84–86), then issues a challenge to Hotspur: "And will, to save blood on either side, / Try fortune with him in a single fight" (5, 1, 100–101). Why would Shakespeare dramatize this fictional proposal? Hal knows it will not be accepted by either side, but the gesture makes him appear noble. Moreover, the King has no reason to accept his son's proposal: "And God befriend us as our cause is just" (5, 1, 121). How ironic that a king who in *Richard II* challenged the will of God now banks on such support under the assumption that whoever holds the throne rules by divine right.

Falstaff's "catechism" (5, 1, 128–42) is vital for several reasons. One, it challenges the concept of honor, and the emptiness that Falstaff describes repudiates Hotspur's pursuit. Two, it shows Sir John's wit, wordplay, and wisdom. Three, it reflects the humanity Hal learns from his "second father" and how it may influence his reign as king. Most importantly, this speech reminds us that Shakespeare never romanticizes warfare. He does portray individuals acting bravely in the midst of slaughter, but he always dramatizes actual combat as barbaric and dehumanizing.

In the next scene, Worcester, again stirring up trouble, urges that Hotspur not be told of the King's inclination to call off the war (5, 2, 1–2), adding that Henry insulted their forces: "He calls 'rebels,' 'traitors,' and will scourge / With haughty arms this hateful name in us" (5, 2, 42–43). But soon Worcester recounts Hal's offer to fight Hotspur one on one, and Vernon adds that the challenge was issued in terms that reflected well on Hal:

> If he outlive the envy of this day,
> England did never owe so sweet a hope
> So much misconstrued in his wantonness. (5, 2, 69–71)

Hotspur, however, remains hungry for glory: "An if we live, we live to tread on kings; / If die, brave death, when princes die with us" (5, 2, 89–90). In some ways Hotspur may be regarded as symbolic of war itself: alluring but horrific.

The battle scenes that follow should be brutal. When Blunt, dressed like the King (a familiar tactic for protection), is killed by Douglas, Falstaff comes across the corpse: "There's honor for you" (5, 3, 35). Seconds later, though, Falstaff adds that among the soldiers he recruited: "There's not three of my hundred and fifty left alive" (5, 3, 39–40). The bloody outcome predicted for those poor souls has come true.

The Prince rushes up to demand a weapon, but Falstaff pulls out a flask. Now fully engaged, Hal has no patience for foolishness: "What, is it a time to jest and dally now?" (5, 3, 59). But Falstaff has his own agenda:

> Give me
> life, which, if I can save, so: if not, honor comes
> unlooked for, and there's an end. (5, 3, 63–65)

We sympathize with his attitude. Yet we also realize that it cannot sustain someone with responsibility, which demands its price, as the Prince demonstrates when he praises his younger brother, John of Lancaster, for his military skill (5, 4, 17–20).

Moments later, Hal rescues his father from attack by Douglas and thereby inspires gratitude from the king: "Thou has redeemed thy lost opinion" (5, 4, 48). Hal, however, offers no filial devotion: "O God, they did me too much injury / That ever said I hearkened for your death" (5, 4, 51–52). No one was more critical of Hal than his father, but Hal does not bother reminding him or us. Instead as his toughness takes hold, he merely fulfills his soldierly duty.

At last the confrontation we have anticipated since the first scene of the play is before us: the fight between Hal and Hotspur (Harry vs. Harry). It is almost certainly fictional, because the manner of Hotspur's death remains unknown. Nevertheless, the scene works wonderfully, especially after Hotspur's unintentionally ironic words set off the contest: "I can no longer brook thy vanities" (5, 4, 75). The individual combat is ferocious, but while it rages, Falstaff encounters his enemy Douglas. We anticipate a struggle, but Sir John falls without even being touched, an act that lends appropriate comic detachment.

After Hotspur dies, Hal offers a gracious tribute: "Fare thee well, great heart. / Ill-weaved ambition, how much art thou shrunk!" (5, 4, 89–90). He recognizes that no matter how bold Hotspur's spirit, the man was, in his own way, a relic. When Hal then spies Falstaff lying motionless, the juxtaposition of the two bodies represents the polarities of Hal's life, but Falstaff is the one he mourns: "O, I should have a heavy miss of thee / If I were much in love with vanity" (5, 4, 107–8). When Hal leaves, though, Falstaff rises and ruminates on the word *counterfeit*, reflecting the theme about the nature of a true king and the emergence of the real Hal.

He adds: "The better part of valor is discretion" (5, 4, 122), justifying his own cowardice, but he also takes time to stab the dead Hotspur to gain reward. When he drags the body and meets Hal, the Prince insists that he himself killed Hotspur, but Falstaff remains unimpressed: "Lord, Lord, how this world is given to lying" (5, 4, 148–49). Lancaster is nonplussed: "This is the strangest tale that ever I heard" (5, 4, 158), to which Hal replies with his most winning line: "This is the strangest fellow, brother John" (5, 4, 159). In that light Falstaff's promise to "live cleanly as a nobleman should do" (5, 4, 168–69) rings delightfully hollow.

In the final scene, Henry IV tries to restore order. He directs Worcester and Vernon to be executed, then promises to weigh the future of other conspirators while dividing responsibilities for military action. He intends to quash the rebellion and simultaneously to restore familial and national order. That vision, however, does not come true, for in *Henry IV, Part 2*, both King Henry and England pay an ever greater price for the usurpation.

If the class is not scheduled to read *Part 2*, here is the moment to explain that while *Part 1* concentrates on Hal's growth and King Henry's temporary triumph, *Part 2* presents death and decay. In particular, it shows the decline and passing of Henry IV and the final cracking of the fissure between Hal and Falstaff. That moment occurs when the Prince becomes King, and Sir John intrudes upon the coronation, only to be expelled by the newly enthroned Henry V. If opportunity is available, consider providing the text of

Hal's order: "I know thee not, old man. Fall to thy prayers" (*Henry IV, Part 2*, 5, 5, 47–70). That moment may be the most heartbreaking in all of Shakespeare.

Henry IV, Part 1 stands as the most enthralling part of Shakespeare's panorama of England in the fifteenth century. The play depicts manipulation, bravery, deceit, nobility, passion, and loss. The result is an extraordinary spectacle made even more compelling by the chorus of the wise, sometimes wistful, sometimes ribald laughter of Falstaff. Specific disputes of that time contributed to the entrance of England into the modern world, but the issues and themes they reflect belong to any age.

A Few Words About the Romances

Toward the end of his career, after he completed ten tragedies, seventeen comedies, and ten histories, Shakespeare turned toward a new dramatic form that includes works known collectively as the romances. They incorporate elements of the other three categories, along with music, dance, and even magic. These new pieces have a didactic quality, as if the playwright was trying to teach about the nature of the world. The elaborate technical demands suggest that these plays were intended to be performed at the indoors Blackfriars Theater, where the audience was more affluent and sophisticated.

The texts share several plot elements, many adapted from folklore. All concern conflict between generations, royal families divided, and children lost over extended periods of time, only to be reunited in scenes of reconciliation. Several stories involve journeys over water, which is seen as both a source of chaos and a sustainer of life. Although major characters endure suffering, the endings are happy, often achieved with help from the supernatural. Furthermore, the good characters are almost always rewarded and the wicked punished.

Thematically, the plays have several points in common. In Shakespeare's more traditional works, trials that the major figures endure result from the interplay between character and circumstance, and personalities and values lead to conflict. In the romances, however, a chain of causality is not always evident, and characters may be victimized through no fault of their own. A sense of mystery pervades, as it does in the tragedies, but here the characters who maintain faith are rewarded by alleviation of their suffering.

One more element should be noted. In all these plays, the most important relationship is between fathers and daughters. In each romance, the father experiences adversity, while the daughter represents hope and regeneration. Although these daughters marry, their love for their husbands seems to reflect feelings for their fathers, a motif familiar from several of the tragedies, notably *King Lear*, in which the title character and his daughter Cordelia, after enduring profound anguish, are reunited in a scene of transcendent beauty.

The father–daughter relationship was a dominant theme of Renaissance literature, but the writing of the romances also coincided with the marriage of Shakespeare's daughter Susanna and the birth of his granddaughter, Elizabeth. Thus this bond may have been especially meaningful to him, embodying what the romances dramatize: the transience of life and the endurance of love.

Chapter Seven

The Tempest

One way to promote interest in this play is to observe that it is generally regarded as the last that Shakespeare completed. He may have had a hand in a few subsequent pieces, but this work is the final one that we credit to him alone. No immediate source has been found, and the plot is comparatively simple, but the story suggests many allegorical perspectives. As you proceed with your discussion, three of the most useful are the artistic, the political, and the familial.

The Tempest is also one of only two plays by Shakespeare that conforms to the classical unities of time, place, and action (the other is *The Comedy of Errors*). The story unfolds in one day, the location is the island, and the action is essentially continuous. More important, we recognize early on that Prospero controls the outcome of everything, and therefore the plot holds little suspense. No matter what alliances and conspiracies form, no matter what individual crises arise, all will resolve happily. What matters is the significance of what we observe.

One other point to consider is that the play was written during the height of the age of exploration. By 1611, when we assume the script was completed, the English had already settled the colony of Jamestown, Virginia. Thus you might take a few minutes to establish dates when the Pilgrims arrived at Plymouth, Massachusetts, or when Spanish explorers reached South America. You might even discuss the interplay between these newcomers and the natives. Students rarely think of Shakespeare as reacting to events of his time, but this play reflects adventures that influenced the world-view of many people.

The play opens amid a ferocious storm, during which several characters reveal their personalities. The boatswain, for instance, has little regard for his social superiors: "Use your authority. If you cannot, give thanks you have lived so long" (1, 1, 24–25). He dismisses ill-used power, a later theme of the play. Gonzalo's response reveals his more placid nature:

> Methinks
> he hath no drowning mark upon him. His
> complexion is perfect gallows. (1, 1, 29–31)

Gonzalo's good-humored faith becomes his hallmark, but how it survives in the world is another matter.

The ugly side of that world is embodied first by Sebastian: "A pox o' your throat, you bawling, blasphemous, incharitable dog!" (1, 1, 41–42), then by Antonio: "Hang, cur, hang, you whoreson, insolent noisemaker!" (1, 1, 44–45). Antonio, we soon learn, usurped the dukedom of Milan from Prospero, and his intolerance for others will be manifested on the island as well, where he and Sebastian undertake another conspiracy. What about the tempest itself? First, it is a product of Prospero's art and a manifestation of his anger. Second, it represents governmental upset in Milan. And third, it embodies the fragmentation of the royal family.

The background to this turmoil is brought out when Miranda solicits her father: "If by your art, my dearest father, you have / Put the wild waters in this roar, allay them" (1, 2, 1–2). She adds: "O, I have suffered / With those that I saw suffer!" (1, 2, 5–6). Here is the sympathy that will distinguish her throughout the play, and we shall wonder from where this quality emerges. Is it inherent in her? Or has she acquired it living in isolation? And how do answers to those questions reflect other human beings and their values?

Prospero then begins a long narrative that he periodically interrupts to ensure that Miranda's attention as well as ours remains focused. The essence is that Prospero became absorbed in his own studies: "I, thus neglecting worldly ends" (1, 2, 109). Into that void stepped his brother, Antonio, who gained control over the state of Milan (1, 2, 84–95). Such power: "in my false brother / Awaked an evil nature" (1, 2, 112–13), and after much political manipulation Prospero was expelled from office. In sum, although Prospero was a legitimate ruler, he failed to fulfill responsibilities bestowed on him by God.

Antonio was then joined in conspiracy by Alonso, King of Naples, described by Prospero as "being an enemy / To me inveterate" (1, 2, 145–46). The two permitted an army to invade Milan, and Prospero and Miranda were carried off. When she asks why Antonio and Alonso did not have them killed, Prospero explains: "Dear, they durst not, / So dear the love my people bore me" (1, 2, 168–69). The pair survived at sea only, in Prospero's words: "By providence divine" (1, 2, 190), which took the form of Gonzalo, who provided necessities as well as Prospero's books.

Prospero's intention, then, is not only to take personal revenge on Antonio but also to restore his city. Now "bountiful Fortune" (1, 2, 213) has brought his enemies to this shore, but Prospero warns that if he fails to take advantage of this opportunity: "my fortunes / Will ever after droop" (1, 2, 218–19). In other words, the universe may be ultimately benign, but individuals are responsible for their own fate.

After allowing Miranda to fall asleep, Prospero summons Ariel, his spirit/slave who dramatizes the storm that he unleashed on Prospero's orders (1, 2, 232–42). All passengers have been rescued, including Ferdinand, Alonso's son, who landed alone (1, 2, 260–62). As Prospero expresses approval (1, 2, 281–82), Ariel recalls promises of liberty, but Prospero's exerting authority reminds Ariel of privileges he enjoys under Prospero's rule. Although Ariel moves through all the elements (1, 2, 302–6), he still retains human feelings, a combination that makes him symbolic of imagination or some other incorporeal attribute.

Prospero, however, is not ready to surrender control of his charge:

> Thou liest, malignant thing. Hast thou forgot
> The foul witch Sycorax, who with age and envy
> Was grown into a hoop? (1, 2, 308–10)

With vengeful pride, Prospero details the imprisonment Ariel suffered. Why should Prospero treat Ariel so harshly? Perhaps Prospero is compensating for his earlier failure as Duke of Milan and in this small kingdom is determined to prevent rebellion, even by one as loyal as Ariel. In any case, Prospero orders Ariel to carry out directives but also promises to fulfill their contract by freeing Ariel in two days (1, 2, 355–56).

Whatever Ariel's nature, he is contrasted by Caliban (nearly an anagram of *cannibal*), whose brutality is evident in his first words:

> As wicked dew as e'er my mother brushed
> With raven's feather from unwholesome fen
> Drop on you both. A southwest blow on you
> And blister you all o'er. (1, 2, 385–88)

Yet he also has a capacity for love, as he recalls Prospero's initial shows of affection:

> When thou cam'st first,
> Thou strok'st me and made much of me, wouldst
>   give me
> Water with berries in 't, and teach me how
> To name the bigger light and how the less,
> That burn by day and night. And then I loved thee,
> And showed thee all the qualities o' th' isle. (1, 2, 397–403)

This passage raises a number of questions. Should we regard Caliban, the son of Sycorax, as representing natives of the American continent who were forced to deal with invaders from European civilization? What was the initial interplay between these cultures? Did the Europeans simply conquer and enslave the natives? Should Europeans, both in the play and historically, be regarded as colonialists and imperialists, who introduced wine and scientific learning to the natives, only to oppress them?

Or does Caliban embody the untutored and violent instincts of humanity? Is his nature essentially bad, and must good be inculcated by the forces of "civilization"? He is at various moments vicious, pathetic, poetic, and naïve. He occasionally offers innocent charm and even affection, but he is also capable of reverting to savagery, as Prospero indicates:

> I have used thee,
> Filth as thou art, with humane care, and lodged thee
> In mine own cell, till thou didst seek to violate
> The honor of my child. (1, 2, 413–18)

Caliban's response is ugly: "Thou didst prevent me. I had peopled else / This isle with Calibans" (1, 2, 420–21).

Miranda insists that she, too, tried to help Caliban:

> I pitied thee,
> Took pains to make thee speak, taught thee each hour
> One thing or other. When thou didst not, savage,
> Know thine own meaning, but wouldst gabble like
> A thing most brutish, I endowed thy purposes
> With words that made them known. (1, 2, 424–30)

She assumes that her understanding of the world is innately superior to that of Caliban. The lessons of society, however, carry risks. In Caliban's words: "You taught me language, and my profit on 't / Is I know how to curse" (1, 2, 437–38). How, then, are we to regard Prospero? As a benign visitor who imparted knowledge? Or as a ruthless conqueror who oppressed those unable to resist him? Ask the class to substitute *European civilization* for *Prospero*, and the magnitude of the question will be apparent.

The final character to be introduced in this scene is Ferdinand, who hears the singing of the invisible Ariel. While the voice haunts Ferdinand, he also notes lyrics that suggest a key theme of the play:

> Nothing of him that doth fade
> But doth suffer a sea change
> Into something rich and strange. (1, 2, 477–79)

Ferdinand believes that these words fit his drowned father, but in fact they apply to several who undergo difficulties, then are altered spiritually and emotionally.

When Miranda sees Ferdinand, she immediately tells her father that she is smitten: "Lord, how it looks about! Believe me, sir, / It carries a brave form. But 'tis a spirit" (1, 2, 489–90). Yet even after Ferdinand responds with equal fervor, Prospero will not make things easy for them. He interrogates Ferdinand about his background so intensely that Miranda becomes upset: "Pity move my father / To be inclined my way" (1, 2, 536–37).

Ferdinand then establishes his own standard:

> O, if a virgin,
> And your affection not gone forth, I'll make you
> The Queen of Naples. (1, 2, 538–40)

Does this stricture suggest a demand for innocence? Are we to accept that principle as legitimate? Prospero sees their mutual attraction but resolves again to make the courtship difficult (1, 2, 542–45). He sentences Ferdinand to hard labor, then at Miranda's protests exerts control: "My foot my tutor?" (1, 2, 569). He even belittles Ferdinand: "To th' most of men this is a Caliban, / And they to him are angels" (1, 2, 584–85). Ferdinand willingly yields, invoking a familiar image from the comedies: "My spirits, as in a dream, are all bound up" (1, 2, 593), but Miranda reassures him: "My father's of a better nature, sir" (1, 2, 606).

As other survivors work their way ashore, they react in characteristic ways. Gonzalo expresses gratitude simply for being alive (2, 1, 1–9), Antonio and Sebastian grouse (2, 1, 46–111), and Alonso mourns the son he believes has drowned (2, 1, 112–19). Sebastian then inflicts more agony on Alonso, blaming him for this voyage that has ended in disaster:

> Sir, you may thank yourself for this great loss,
> That would not bless our Europe with your daughter,
> But rather lose her to an African. (2, 1, 131–33)

We note that Sebastian is Alonso's brother and thus a rival for his throne, just as Antonio sought Prospero's.

The most interesting passage is Gonzalo's vision (2, 1, 162–71) of what he calls the "Golden Age" (2, 1, 184). His utopian reflection is based on faith in man's natural goodness, but the remarks of Antonio and Sebastian form a rude chorus. Sebastian comments: "No marrying 'mong his subjects?" (2, 1, 181), to which Antonio replies: "None, man, all idle: whores and knaves" (2, 1, 182). Just as Caliban represents brutality in nature, so Antonio and Sebastian are a parallel source of corruption in civilization. As long as these forces exist, Gonzalo's dream remains unrealistic.

As Ariel influences Alonso to sleep, Antonio and Sebastian confer. Antonio drops hints: "My strong imagination sees a crown / Dropping upon thy head" (2, 1, 230–31). Sebastian, always the follower, is comically slow in understanding: "Thou dost snore distinctly. / There's meaning in thy snores" (2, 1, 243–44). Finally Antonio loses patience and clarifies his intention:

> O, that you bore
> The mind that I do, what a sleep were this
> For your advancement! Do you understand me? (2, 1, 304–6)

At last Sebastian grasps the implication, and Antonio reminds him of the benefits of usurpation: "My brother's servants / Were then my fellows; now they are my men" (2, 1, 314–15).

When Sebastian maintains doubt: "But, for your conscience?" (2, 1, 316), Antonio has a ready answer: "Ay, sir, where lies that?" (2, 1, 317). In the diatribe that follows (2, 1, 317–31), he resists ethical restraint. He thereby aligns himself with Iago in *Othello*, Edmund in *King Lear*, and other Machiavels (see chapter 4 on *Othello*'s Iago in *Introducing Shakespeare's Tragedies: A Guide for Teachers*). He thinks only of himself, and his will dominates his other feelings. Yet as far as Antonio knows, he has no chance of rescue. Thus this conspiracy emerges simply from instinct, irrespective of purpose, and stands as one more contradiction of Gonzalo's ideal society.

Antonio and Sebastian draw swords to carry out Alonso's murder, but Ariel awakens Gonzalo, who rouses Alonso, and the conspiracy is temporarily abated. Antonio and Sebastian concoct a lie about hunting animals, but the image that stays with us is of two vicious men ready to kill to gain nonexistent jurisdiction. We also remember Gonzalo's closing remark about Ferdinand: "Heavens keep him from these beasts" (2, 1, 373).

A comic analogue to this machination springs up in the next scene. First Caliban enters, cursing Prospero with poetry that is cruel yet graphic (2, 2, 1–17). We recognize his energy, but he lacks the intellect to guide it. Hearing Trinculo, Caliban imagines him a spirit of Prospero's and so hides under a cloak. Trinculo in turn cannot tell what Caliban is but postulates whether the creature would turn a profit back in England. Here the imperialist spirit is at work.

When the drunken Stephano joins them, he and Trinculo gradually realize that the two of them are alive (2, 2, 106–17). The more they speak, the more ridiculous we understand them to be, but Caliban remains convinced that their origins are divine: "That's a brave god and bears celestial liquor. / I will kneel to him" (2, 2, 121–22). Before long, he is eager to serve: "I'll show thee every fertile inch o' th' island, and I will kiss thy foot. I prithee, be my god" (2, 2, 154–55).

Does the play suggest that as a "primitive" Caliban prefers to be ruled? Are we to accept that peoples everywhere who were conquered by Europeans sought to be controlled? Here Caliban willingly exchanges one ruler for another, and this alliance is a parody of the other. Stephano, like Antonio, is the instigator (2, 2, 173–83); Trinculo, like Sebastian, is the follower; and Caliban, like Gonzalo, sings about freedom.

As Ferdinand works to win Miranda, the difficulty of the task is partially assuaged by his devotion to her: "The mistress which I serve quickens what's dead / And makes my labors pleasures" (3, 1, 6–7). He may be regarded as the archetypal Renaissance suitor, enduring trials to win the hand of the woman he loves. When Miranda enters, she is so enraptured that she offers to help him: "If you'll sit down, / I'll bear your logs the while" (3, 1, 27–28). Her devotion moves even Prospero: "Poor worm, thou art infected" (3, 1, 38).

Yet he is determined that until their wedding both Miranda and Ferdinand remain pure. Perhaps he is exerting paternal authority, or perhaps he is maintaining the hierarchical control he surrendered in Milan. Ferdinand, too, is in love, and although he admits to knowing many other women (3, 1, 49–56), he prizes Miranda for her purity:

> But you, O you,
> So perfect and so peerless, are created
> Of every creature's best. (3, 1, 56–58)

He is taken with her lack of worldliness, for she is free from the taint of society that has ruined other relationships. What are we to make of such standards for a young woman?

Also noteworthy in this scene is Miranda's innocence: "Nor have I seen / More that I may call men than you, good friend" (3, 1, 61–62). *Friend* seems in an odd word, but for these two it fits, because they are indeed friends before they become lovers. Meanwhile Ferdinand offers appropriate words from a lovesick swain: "The very instant that I saw you did / My heart fly to your service" (3, 1, 76–77). Even Prospero is moved by their mutual affection: "Heavens rain grace / On that which breed between 'em" (3, 1, 90–91). But before that marriage can be carried out, he has other business to complete.

Part of his work is to thwart the two conspiracies that have formed against him. As Trinculo and Stephano bicker, Caliban urges them to establish some kind of order: "Lo, how he mocks me! Wilt thou let him, my lord?" (3, 2, 33–34). He even has a political agenda about Prospero: "I say by sorcery he got this isle" (3, 2, 59). The invisible Ariel's interruptions drive the trio to distraction, but Caliban remains a puzzling presence. He is gullible for trusting these buffoons, but he also advocates violence on Prospero (3, 2, 97–100).

The most surprising aspect about Caliban, though, is his insight. Here he describes Prospero:

> Remember
> First to possess his books, for without them
> He's but a sot, as I am, nor hath not
> One spirit to command. (3, 2, 100–103)

The other, even more remarkable moment occurs when music Ariel plays frightens Trinculo and Stephano, and Caliban steps up to comfort them: "Be not afeard. This isle is full of noises, / Sounds and sweet airs that give delight and hurt not" (3, 2, 148–49). The rest of the speech is equally eloquent. Is this the voice of a "primitive"? Or is he Shakespeare's portrait of raw, untutored humankind, with the capacity for both good and evil?

The more dangerous conspiracy resurfaces in the next scene, as Alonso broods over what he believes is the death of his son (3, 3, 10–12). His preoccupation leads Antonio and Sebastian to persist in their plan to murder him, but the plot is interrupted by what are described as "several strange shapes" (3, 3, 24) that provide a banquet. Gonzalo is characteristically grateful for the sustenance (3, 3, 34–41), but just as quickly the images vanish amid thunder and lightning. At every moment we feel Prospero's control.

What follows is a litany of accusations by Ariel, particularly the usurpation of Prospero's throne and the promise of further punishment for purgation of their sins (3, 3, 88–101). While Prospero approves the performance: "They now are in my power" (3, 3, 110), Alonso vows to search for his son: "I'll seek him deeper than e'er plummet sounded, / And with him there lie mudded" (3, 3, 122–23). The line implies that he will commit suicide. Gonzalo, however, strikes the note of forgiveness that dominates the last two acts:

> Their great guilt,
> Like poison given to work a great time after,
> Now 'gins to bite the spirits. (3, 3, 127–29)

It continues when Prospero at last takes pity on Ferdinand:

> All thy vexations
> Were but my trials of thy love, and thou
> Hast strangely stood the test. (4, 1, 5–7)

In this context *strangely* means *well*, but Prospero also maintains his one premarriage reservation:

> But
> If thou dost break her virgin-knot before
> All sanctimonious ceremonies may
> With full and holy rite be ministered,
> No sweet aspersion shall the heavens let fall
> To make this contract grow. (4, 1, 15–20)

Once more Ferdinand agrees (4, 1, 25–33), so we wonder whose obsession is at the heart of this condition: Ferdinand's, Prospero's, or Shakespeare's? And does it imply that the ideal woman is without experience, sexual or otherwise? In creating this magical world, is Shakespeare imposing some fantasy of his own?

Prospero then orders Ariel to summon the "rabble" to participate in the marriage ceremony but again reminds Ferdinand: "Be more abstemious, / Or else goodnight your vow" (4, 1, 58–59), to which Ferdinand complies without hesitation: "The white cold virgin snow upon my heart / Abates the ardor of my liver" (4, 1, 61–62). The liver was thought to be the source of such passions. As goddesses from mythology gather to bless the marriage and ensure fertility, Ceres prevents one from joining: Venus, along with her son Cupid (4, 1, 95–100), an omission in line with Prospero's orders.

As the singing and dancing are underway, providing opportunity, you should note, for imaginative directors and musicians to create a phantasmagoria for the stage, Prospero suddenly interrupts the ceremony:

> I had forgot that foul conspiracy
> Of the beast Caliban and his confederates
> Against my life. (4, 1, 155–57)

He dismisses the performers and in partial explanation for the display of temper that frightens Ferdinand and Miranda offers one of the most celebrated passages in Shakespeare.

The first part reflects on the curious fate of stage players:

> These our actors,
> As I foretold you, were all spirits and
> Are melted into air, into thin air. (4, 1, 165–67)

As they slip from role to role, they embody the transience of life:

> And like the baseless fabric of this vision,
> The cloud-capped towers, the gorgeous palaces,
> The solemn temples, the great globe itself,
> Yea, all which it inherit, shall dissolve,
> And, like this insubstantial pageant faded,
> Leave not a rack behind. (4, 1, 168–73)

As he mentions the evanescence of the stage, Prospero seems to suggest that all creative work fades, even Shakespeare's. (The "great globe itself" no doubt refers to his home theater.) Here is a moment to ask who among your students has been involved in a stage production, then to inquire of the participants how they felt after the final performance of a run, when the set was struck and the stage was left empty. They will likely put Shakespeare's sentiments into their own words.

The next three lines are the most famous:

> We are such stuff
> As dreams are made on, and our little life
> Is rounded with a sleep. (4, 1, 173–75)

The comparison between human existence and the life of the theater is familiar from other plays. Macbeth speaks of life as a "poor player / That struts and frets his hour upon the stage" (5, 5, 27–28), and in *As You Like It*, Jaques proclaims: "All the world's a stage" (2, 7, 146). The implication is that given the brevity of human existence, we must show compassion for human weakness.

Ariel then brings word of the humiliations suffered by Caliban and his cohorts (4, 1, 190–205), inviting Prospero to inflict more pain: "And as with age his body uglier grows, / So his mind cankers" (4, 1, 214–15). He is not yet ready to permit forgiveness. When Trinculo and Stephano arrive, they are pained more deeply by the loss of their liquor (4, 1, 233), but that is soon forgotten when they are beset by spirits in the shape of "dogs and hounds" (4, 1, 281). The resulting chaos leaves Prospero to his final victory: "At this hour / Lies at my mercy all mine enemies" (4, 1, 291–92). How he exerts that power is a final theme of the play.

As act 5 opens, Ariel reminds Prospero of the state of the conspirators:

> Your charm so strongly works
> 'em
> That if you now beheld them, your affections
> Would become tender. (5, 1, 21–24)

In one of the warmest moments in all of Shakespeare, Prospero asks: "Dost thou think so, spirit?" (5, 1, 25), and Ariel's answer resounds throughout all the plays: "Mine would, sir, were I human" (5, 1, 26). This exchange brings out Ariel's complicated nature: part human, part supernatural. Prospero agrees: "And mine shall" (5, 1, 27), then adds a vital note: "The rarer action is / In virtue than in vengeance" (5, 1, 35–36).

We think of Romeo, pursuing revenge after Mercutio slays Tybalt; Hamlet, trapped by the revenge ethic of his society; and Macbeth, possessed by a longing for power that he cannot resist. We think of the sequence of history plays, in which ambition and intrafamily rivalry dominate England for nearly a century. *The Tempest* shows us all these forces of destruction, but they are controlled by Prospero.

Now he offers a long soliloquy in which he summons his powers, then prepares to leave them aside. The last few lines are especially touching: "But this rough magic / I here abjure" (5, 1, 59–60). Numerous commentators have speculated that these words reflect Shakespeare's farewell to his own kind of magic, that of artistic creation. We cannot be sure, but in concert with "Our revels now are ended" from act 4 and the Epilogue, we feel the possibility that Shakespeare knew that his career was nearing its close.

Ariel escorts Alonso, Gonzalo, and the others before Prospero, who sends Ariel for the rest of the ship's crew, then addresses the royals and their company. He praises Gonzalo, then lambasts the others, but true to his word, Prospero shows pity, even to Antonio: "I do forgive thee, / Unnatural though thou art" (5, 1, 88–89). Prospero does insist, however, on his restoration to the throne (5, 1, 149–54). Antonio says nothing, so we can only guess whether he is chastened.

One source of tension remains, which Prospero extends by speaking of Miranda and Ferdinand as though they are lost. Alonso seems truly repentant: "O heavens, that they were living both in Naples, / The King and Queen there!" (5, 1, 174–75). At this confession, Prospero reveals Ferdinand and Miranda behind a curtain playing chess, a sight that moves even Sebastian: "A most high miracle!" (5, 1, 208). Why chess? Perhaps the game signals the end of the war between Milan and Naples, just as the forthcoming marriage suggests the uniting of the two families.

As Miranda witnesses all these people brought together, she is inspired:

> How many goodly creatures are there here!
> How beauteous mankind is! O, brave new world
> That has such people in 't! (5, 1, 216–18)

Most students will recognize in these lines the title of Aldous Huxley's famous novel, but more important is Prospero's dark response: "'Tis new to thee" (5, 1, 219). He has seen too much and knows too much to be swept up in the moment. Despite all the miracles he has wrought on the island, human nature is unalterable, so Miranda still has much to learn.

Alonso's reaction is one of the crucial lines in the play: "But, O, how oddly it will sound that I / Must ask my child forgiveness!" (5, 1, 234–35). Here is another speech that reverberates throughout Shakespeare. Many of his plays dramatize conflict between generations, the clash of old values and new, and how often parents sow seeds of destruction for their offspring. We think of Romeo and Juliet, Hamlet, Othello and Desdemona, King Lear, Baptista, Egeus, Shylock, Henry IV, and many others. If one theme may be said to permeate Shakespeare's oeuvre, it is that of the younger generation attempting to heal wounds cause by the older.

The boatswain returns to relate his fantastic story (5, 1, 277–90), after which Ariel whispers to Prospero: "Was 't well done?" (5, 1, 291). Now Prospero at last utters the words for which Ariel has been waiting: "Thou shalt be free" (5, 1, 292). Stephano, however, maintains his customary swagger:

> Every man shift for all the rest, and let no
> man take care for himself, for all is but fortune.
> Coraggio, bully monster, coraggio. (5, 1, 310–12).

Even Caliban realizes that he has been a fool:

> What a thrice-double ass
> Was I to take this drunkard for a god
> And worship this dull fool! (5, 1, 352–54)

Yet we see no sign that events have modified his character, and he remains outside the bounds of civilization. Nevertheless, the calming of the tempest as promised by Prospero (5, 1, 364–69) and the freeing of Ariel (5, 1, 376–79) do represent the reestablishment of order and the expression of exoneration.

The Epilogue opens and closes with lines that appear to come directly from Shakespeare himself. First: "Now my charms are all o'erthrown, / And what strength I have 's mine own" (Epilogue, 1–2). He seems to be asking to be allowed to retreat from public life. Second: "As you from crimes would pardoned be, / Let your indulgence set me free" (Epilogue, 19–20). However he might have offended his audiences, he asks forgiveness.

Indeed, forgiveness is at the heart of this play, as it is in most of Shakespeare's works. This particular story suggests that evil can never be eradicated, but at the same time Shakespeare's view seems founded on the conviction that humanity is ultimately redeemable. Whatever struggles we undergo, whether political, social, emotional, or artistic, grappling with them helps make existence meaningful.

Afterword

I hope the material here has been useful. As I indicated earlier, I have only introduced our subject, but again, my intended audience is instructors who work with beginners, and experience has taught me that the approaches I've advocated do succeed.

Decades ago, when I was teaching at prep school, I announced to a tenth-grade class that the next book on our reading list was Shakespeare's *Julius Caesar*. Groans filled the room, amid pleas to the effect that couldn't we read something else, *anything* else? A few weeks later, after we finished the play, the same class pleaded to read something else, *anything* else by Shakespeare, and soon we agreed that *Romeo and Juliet* would be ideal. I can't remember a more satisfying moment in my career.

Oh yes. *Romeo and Juliet* was a hit, too.

To conclude, I shall immodestly suggest a few other books of mine that may prove of interest. One is the companion to this volume, *Introducing Shakespeare's Tragedies: A Guide for Teachers*. Those interested in the rest of Shakespeare's oeuvre might try *Shakespeare the Playwright: A Companion to the Complete Tragedies, Histories, Comedies, and Romances* (1991). Those who seek commentary about specific themes should look at *The Plays of Shakespeare: A Thematic Guide* (2000), while those interested in the history plays (specifically, the Henriad) should read *Political Animal: An Essay on the Character of Shakespeare's Henry V* (2014). Finally, for those who enjoy puzzles and other diversions, I recommend *Bardgames: The Shakespeare Quiz Book* (2011).

Good luck.

About the Author

Victor L. Cahn is professor emeritus of English at Skidmore College, where he taught courses in Shakespeare, modern drama, the history of drama, and expository writing. He also taught at Mercersburg Academy, Pomfret School, Phillips Exeter Academy, and Bowdoin College. He was recently profiled in *300 Best Professors*.

In addition to seven books on Shakespeare, he has written *Beyond Absurdity: The Plays of Tom Stoppard*; *Gender and Power in the Plays of Harold Pinter*; *Conquering College: A Guide for Undergraduates* and the memoir *Classroom Virtuoso* (both published by Rowman & Littlefield); *Polishing Your Prose* (with Steven M. Cahn); and *Walking Distance: Remembering Classic Episodes from Classic Television*. His articles and reviews have appeared in such varied publications as *Modern Drama, Literary Review, Chronicle of Higher Education, New York Times*, and *Variety*.

Dr. Cahn is the author of numerous plays produced Off-Broadway and regionally: *Roses in December, Embraceable Me, Fit to Kill, Dally with the Devil, A Dish for the Gods, Sheepskin, Romantic Trapezoid, Villainous Company, Getting the Business, Bottom of the Ninth,* and *Sherlock Solo,* a one-man show that he performed. Other scripts of his have been presented throughout the Capital Region of New York, where he has taken leading roles in works by Shakespeare, Shaw, Coward, Pinter, Ayckbourn, Simon, Gurney, and Knott.

www.ingramcontent.com/pod-product-compliance
Lightning Source LLC
Chambersburg PA
CBHW020753230426
43665CB00009B/573